First printing 2002
1 2 3 4 5 6 7 8 9 10   07 06 05 04 03 02
Printed in the United States of America

Editorial Director: Lois Keffer
Edited by Susan Martins Miller

Art Direction by Mike Riester
Cover Design by Peter Schmidt and Scot McDonald, Granite Design
Interior Design by Dana Sherrer, iDesignEtc.
Illustrations by Aline Heiser

ISBN 0781438373

Table of Contents

Introduction

Ms. Brandt told the kids in her classroom that she was going to announce a "special" news bulletin in the coming week. The class exploded in a loud cheer. The kids knew what Ms. Brandt meant—a new bulletin board! They couldn't wait to find out all about it. The next week came and class was about to begin. Everyone knew it was the morning of the "special news bulletin." All morning the children pelted Ms. Brandt with questions. "What are we going to get to do? Can I help? Will we hang stuff like the last time? What will the Bible story be about? I have an idea; can I share it?"

Have you ever heard children begging to know about the next bulletin board? Well, Ms. Brandt did! She had discovered a secret: *Interactive* bulletin boards, where teaching and learning are off the wall! Literally!

Interactive bulletin boards are just that—interactive! These bulletin boards go far beyond a display in the classroom or hallway decoration. They display works that are *in progress*. They display what kids have learned and chart their growth in fun and engaging ways. Kids help create these bulletin boards with their own hands and are actively involved in making, hanging and maintaining their learning space. By helping to construct bulletin boards, kids feel invested in them, and they're proud and eager to display what they've learned.

Interactive boards give added learning space to your hallway or classroom. You can use an interactive board for a mini lesson that kids work on for a couple of weeks. Or use one to reinforce concepts taught from a Bible story. However you use them, teaching off the wall—or the ceiling or floor—engages kids in a whole new style of learning. You may find yourself less worried about how a bulletin board "looks" and more enthused about what kids are learning from it—and excited to see how God is leaving a lasting "print" on their lives through something as unlikely as a bulletin board!

What is a Godprint?

A Godprint is the evidence that "God was here!" As we come to know God, we grow to love him and want to be like him. With his transforming touch, God makes us more like himself every day. We gain new attitudes and character qualities. Noah had **confidence** because he believed God's promise. Elijah had **faith**, and fire struck Mt. Carmel because God was there. Having seen God work on his behalf before, David had **courage** to conquer a giant! These attributes are Godprints—touches of God that changed lives!

Whether you're an experienced teacher or a novice, it's great to know that it's not up to you to transform a life. Only God can do that. These interactive bulletin boards with mini lessons offer a place where those life-changing encounters with God can happen.

How should I use this book?

You can use this book in a way that meets the specific needs of your teaching time and space and the size and ability of your group. Use the ideas in any order that you choose. Build lessons around them or use just the mini lessons provided here. Observe special holidays, or supplement themes that your pastor is exploring. It's time to think "out of the box"—to experience the fun of off-the-wall thinking and learning!

For each bulletin board, we've provided:

- a sketch of what a finished board might look like;
- a "Get List" that tells you everything you need;
- step-by-step instructions for assembling the board;
- a mini lesson you can use to introduce kids to the board in one lesson or over a period of several weeks;
- a reproducible page of patterns or handouts for the kids; and
- spin-offs—ideas to spark your own creativity to adapt the concept to your own interests or use it with other Bible stories and verses.

Each bulletin board has a Godprint and a Bible verse, so keep a Bible handy for every lesson. Feel free to use other verses and adapt the design. A set of stencil letters will be a great help. Your finished bulletin board does not have to look exactly like the picture you see in the book.

The mini lessons suggest ways the kids can interact with the bulletin board—even to help construct it as part of your time together. The mini lessons are designed to help kids understand the Bible verse and express ways that they can apply its truth in their own lives.

Look for Boldface Print!

Many teachers like the option of a scripted lesson. Bold print offers a "script" you can follow while giving your lesson. Or you may choose to use it as an outline for your own words. Use them at your leisure!

Are you ready? Then…

So roll out the butcher paper!
Grab the scalloped-edge scissors!
Get your kids together for off-the-wall
learning they'll never forget!

Chapter 1

Things that POP SPRING and REACH OUT to touch you!

Creating bulletin boards with three-dimensional depth doesn't have to be hard. Here are a few of the simple ways you'll find in this chapter:

• Staple lightweight chicken wire onto the bulletin board so that it bows out. Shape it however you'd like. Stuff the shape with loosely wadded newspaper.

• Attach strips of heavyweight paper or poster board so that they protrude from the bulletin board.

• Attach three-dimensional objects such as lightweight baskets, small tree branches, picture frames, toys or party decorations to the board.

• Place artificial plants, children's furniture or garden statues in front of the bulletin board.

• Hang items from the ceiling in front of the board. Tie thread to paper clips and hook the clips onto the framing of the ceiling tile.

Think beyond staples and pushpins. Try some of these ideas for attaching items to your board:

- Double-sided tape
- Hot glue (easily removes from surfaces with a hair dryer and paper towel)
- Rubber cement (easily rubs off most surfaces)
- Plasti-Tak® or Poster Putty®
- Krazy Glue® (just remember, it's permanent!)
- Glue sticks
- Paper clips and binder clips

Don't Blow Your Top

Godprint

self-control

Helping kids control selfish impulses encourages them to honor God in their attitude, actions and behavior.

Purpose

CONTROLLING OUR ANGER HONORS GOD. KIDS WILL LEARN TO RECOGNIZE WHAT MAKES THEM ANGRY, LOOK FOR WARNING SIGNS WHEN THEY'RE GETTING ANGRY, AND WHAT TO DO TO COOL OFF AND KEEP FROM BLOWING THEIR TOPS.

Get List

- Green and brown bulletin board paper
- Orange, red and yellow tissue paper
- Pushpins or tiny nails
- Chicken wire
- Staple gun
- Masking tape
- Poster board
- Oatmeal container
- Construction paper
- Reproduce magma, warning signs and ice cubes from page 11
- Plasti-Tak®

Construction Site: Build a volcano.

Kids will attach magma, warning signs and ice cubes.

1 Cover the board with green bulletin board paper. In the center of the board toward the top use push pins or tiny nails to securely attach a small cardboard oatmeal container. This will be the opening to the top cone of the volcano.

2 Use chicken wire to construct the outside of the volcano. Start around the top of the oatmeal container and mold it into an outward triangular shape. Bend the bottom ends of the chicken wire under. Attach the chicken wire with a staple gun.

3 Cover the chicken wire with brown bulletin board paper. Fill the cone with tissue paper. You may wish to position a flashlight in the container so that it shines up through the tissue paper.

4 Make the title, "Don't Blow Your Top!" by cutting out letters from construction paper and attaching them to a strip of poster board. Use staples or push pins to attach the poster board so that it bows out. Cut letters from construction paper to spell out: "God can help you keep your top from blowing!" Place the phrase just below the heading.

5 Cut out more construction paper headers.

- On the left side of the volcano put the words, "My Warning Signs."
- On the volcano put the words: "Things That Make My Magma Rise."
- On the right side of the volcano put the words: "Cool Off!"

Mini Lesson

People who study volcanos are called volcanologists. They try to predict when a volcano will explode. They watch for signs such as a rise in temperature, an earthquake, a rise in pressure and hot lava. These are signs that a volcano might blow its top, and volcanologists can warn people to move. In some cases they can drill vents to help the volcano cool off and prevent it from blowing its top at all.

Give each child a copy of the reproducible. **When we become angry we're a lot like a volcano. What are some things that make you really hot? Write these on your magma.** Kids may say things such as, people don't listen to me; I've been embarrassed; someone made fun of me; I was blamed for something I didn't do.

Spin-Offs: You can use a similar set-up with an iceberg. Change the colors. The tip of the cone becomes the tip of the iceberg. Add cellophane for a water effect. When we're angry we see just the top of the iceberg. **What are things that build up your anger underneath your iceberg?** You can also use the volcano or iceberg with the following Bible stories:

• Joseph keeps his cool (Genesis 37–45).
• Moses loses his cool (Exodus 32).

Ask a volunteer to read James 1:19–20 from a Bible. **God wants to help us stay cool when we see the warning signs that we're getting angry. What are some of your warning signs? Write these on your warning sign.** Kids may say things such as, clinching teeth; sweaty palms; face gets red; voice get louder; crying.

What are some ways that you can cool off when you feel your volcano about to blow? Write these things on your ice cube. Kids may say things such as, talk it out with God, pray; talk to someone; play music; doodle; jump rope; hit a balloon.

Have kids cut out the three parts of the reproducible, then show how to assemble the ice cubes. Attach the magna, warning signs and ice cubes to the board under the appropriate headings with Plasti-Tak®.

• **When you feel as though your volcano is about to blow, what will you do?**
• **Show me one thing you can do to vent when you're feeling steamed.**
• **Who do you honor and who do you help when you keep your anger under control?**

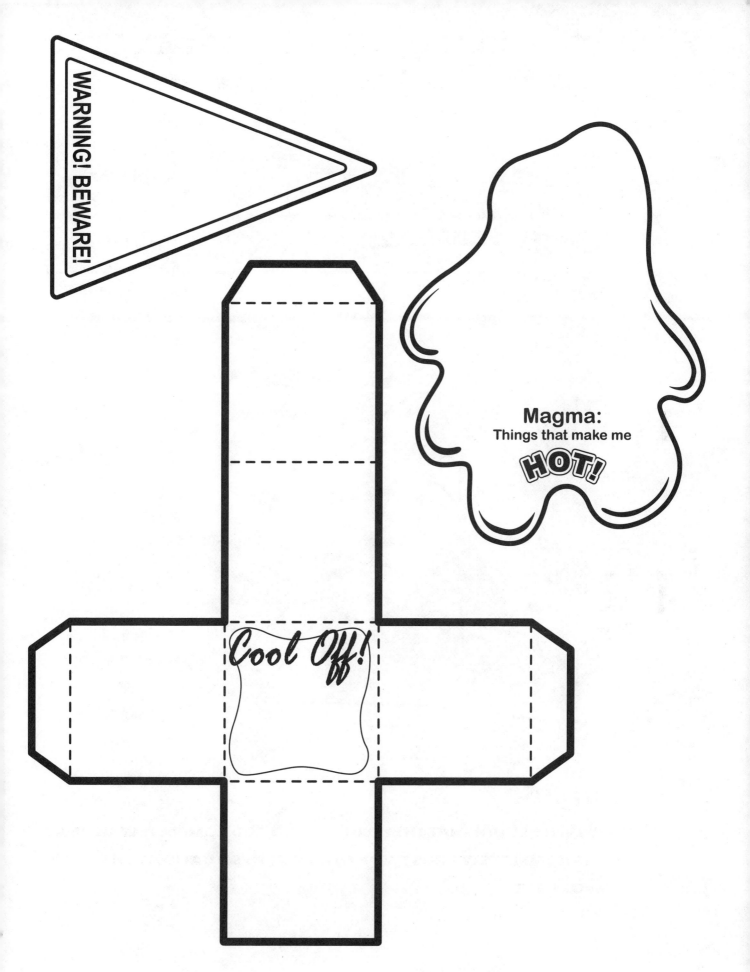

Trusting God with BIG Situations

John 14:1

Do not let your hearts be troubled. Trust in God; trust also in me.

trust

As kids get bigger, so do their problems! But nothing is too big for God to handle. Understanding that God is trustworthy builds a foundation for kids' growing faith.

Purpose

KIDS WILL LEARN THAT THEY CAN RELY ON GOD COMPLETELY, BECAUSE HE IS COMPLETELY TRUSTWORTHY, EVEN IN SITUATIONS THAT SEEM IMPOSSIBLE.

Get List

- Chicken wire
- Twine
- Thin brown yarn or thread
- Men's sandals
- Newspaper
- Liquid starch
- Brown and gray tempera paints
- Overhead or opaque projector
- Bulletin board paper
- Markers, paints or pastels
- Masking tape
- Brown paper lunch sacks
- Constructin paper
- Reproduce page 15

Construction Site: Build a 3-D Goliath. Kids will add lunch bag stones.

1 Ask a man wearing jeans to pose as a mold. Loosely press chicken wire around each leg from the knee to the bottom of the foot to get the shape of a large leg. Use twine to secure the edges of the wire together. Let your friend step out of the cast. Stuff each leg cast with newspaper.

2 Dip strips of newspaper into liquid starch. Run the wet strips between your index and middle fingers to get rid of excess starch. Lay wet strips over the chicken wire until each leg is covered. Let dry. Repeat with another layer if necessary. Paint legs with brown or tan tempera paint. Attach short strands of brown yarn or thread to the leg for hair if you wish.

3 This project will extend about three feet out onto the floor and go all the way up to the ceiling. Measure the width of the space you plan to use. Then cut a piece of brown bulletin board paper as wide as you need and long enough to start at the ceiling and run down the wall. Cut another piece that will extend several feet from the wall on the floor.

4 Use an overhead or opaque projector to trace the "fallen Goliath" pattern (on page 15) onto the paper you measured for the wall. Use markers, paints or pastels to complete the background as desired. Securely attach the finished background onto the wall with tape, staples, glue or rubber cement. Crumple the paper you measured for the floor. Then flatten it and tape it firmly to the floor.

5 Attach Goliath's completed 3-D legs to the wall background so that his legs appear to pop out of the picture. Use staples, tape or hot glue to attach the legs to the background. Support with 3-D rocks as needed (see below). Place men's sandals onto Goliath's feet.

6 To create 3-D rocks, crumple newspaper into medium- to large-sized balls. Secure the shape with masking tape. Paint with gray and/or brown tempera paint. Let dry. Place a few of the rocks on the floor around Goliath's legs. Tie twine around one rock and hang it from the ceiling so it appears to be flying toward Goliath.

7 Cut construction paper letters for the title of the board and tape or staple the title along the top. Add the Bible Verse. (See page 15 for sample.)

Mini Lesson

Did you know that Goliath really was a giant? The Bible tells us about him in 1 Samuel 17:4–7. Goliath was over nine feet tall! That's a common height for the ceiling in many buildings. You may wish to point this fact out to the kids to give them a concrete reference. **The armor he wore weighed about 125 pounds! Just the tip of his spear weighed 15 pounds—as much as two gallons of milk. Can you imagine how large Goliath must have been just to be able to carry his armor and spear?** Give the kids a few minutes to share their thoughts.

Saul, the king of the Israelites, and all the people were terrified Goliath. For 40 days, Goliath challenged the Israelites. For 40 days the Israelites were afraid and did nothing. Have you ever been terrified before? Have you ever faced a really big problem? Invite those who wish to share. Then invite a child to read John 14:1 from a Bible.

Spin-Offs: Children can easily add button-people (see Conquer the Mountain, page 20) as Philistines or Israelites. Each button person can have a speech balloon the children add as well. You could make a more generic giant to talk about accomplishing hard things and use one of these stories:

- Gideon and 300 men defeat the Midianites (Judges 7).
- Caleb and Joshua are faithful spies (Numbers 13–14).

Give each child a brown lunch sack, a slip of writing paper and newspaper. Have them write "I trust God" on their bags. Then say, **Think about a problem in your life that you want to trust God to take care of for you. Write or draw a picture of that problem on your writing paper. When you're done, crumple it up and put it inside your bag. Then stuff your bag half full with wadded newspaper.** Demonstrate this process.

No problem is too big for God! When Saul and all the people were terrified, God sent a young boy named David to the Israelite camp. God gave David the courage to face Goliath, even when the entire Israelite army ran in fear.

David trusted God. He told Goliath, "I come against you in the name of the Lord"(1 Samuel 17:45). **And guess what? God used David to get rid of the big problem! David conquered the big problem with a small stone and his trust in God. Let's add our stones to the bulletin board.** Help kids fasten their lunch sack stones to the display.

We all have problems in our lives. Some are big and some are small. But no matter what the problem is, we can trust God to take care of them. Every time you see your stone, you can remember that no problem is too big for God!

Trust God in BIG Situations!

Do not let your hearts
be troubled.
Trust in God;
trust also in me.   John 14:1

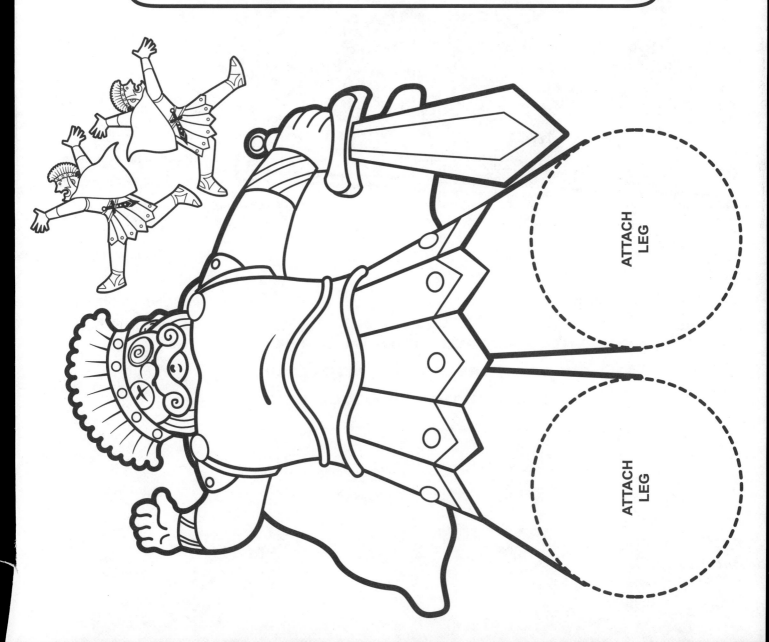

ATTACH LEG

ATTACH LEG

God, the Driver of Hope

Bible Verse

Psalm 25:5

Guide me in your truth and teach me, for you are God my Savior, and my hope is in you all day long.

Godprint

hope

You can make a honking difference in kids' lives by helping them gain confidence that God is in control. Help them grip the fact that God steers their futures and will bring good from all things.

Purpose

KIDS WILL RECOGNIZE TIMES WHEN THEY FEEL OUT OF CONTROL. THEY'LL ALSO LEARN THAT HOPE RESTS IN THE GRIP OF GOD, WHO IS ALWAYS IN CONTROL.

Get List

- Old road maps
- Old steering wheel or foil
- Black construction paper
- Black bulletin board paper
- Pair of rubber gloves
- Stapler and staples
- Cotton balls or polyester stuffing
- Wire and nails
- Push pins
- Markers
- Bibles
- Yarn
- Cardboard
- Reproduce page 19

Construction Site: Build two cars that have steering wheels. Reproducible art is provided for kids to add to the map background.

1 Cover the bulletin board with old road maps. Cut a large car and small car out of the black bulletin board paper. Attach them to the bulletin board with staples so that the larger car is towards the top left and the smaller car is to the bottom right.

2 Use an old steering wheel or make one from foil. Attach the steering wheel to the larger car with wire and push pins. Cut a smaller steering wheel from cardboard. Punch a hole in the center of the steering wheel with a screwdriver and attach it to the smaller car by inserting a large-headed nail in the center of the wheel. The hole cannot be larger than the head of the nail. It should spin when attached.

3 Cut from construction paper the heading, "God's Steering Wheel" and attach the heading above the large car. Cut out the other heading, "My Steering Wheel" and attach above the small car.

4 Stuff the rubber gloves with cotton balls or polyester stuffing and tie them closed. Attach the gloves to the steering wheel on the large car.

5 Make photocopies of pages 19 and cut apart the pieces.

Mini Lesson

- How many of you have ever watched a car race on television?
- When you saw a car crash, how did you feel?

Sometimes life can seem out of control like a car zig-zagging down the road. For example, life might feel out of control when your family decides to move. Life might seem out of control when you find out your grandpa died, or if your best friend was mean to you.

Let's think about times when life seemed out of control for you, your family or a friend. Hand out the photocopied steering wheels and markers. **Write about something that happened that caused you to feel out of control.** Allow time for writing or drawing.

Many times when things seem out of control we feel anxious, worried, angry or hopeless. We try to grab the "steering wheel" of our lives and try to take control and do things our own way. Have the kids pin the steering wheels on the board.

Spin-Offs: Use this bulletin board with the following stories:
- God's people lose the map and wander in the desert (Numbers 14).
- God has a great plan for Joseph (Genesis 41).
- Jonah takes a wrong turn (Jonah).

All of these things might make us feel pretty desperate. When *we* steer our car and we don't let *God* be the driver of our lives, we might act out or become very angry. We might drive our car into the garage so we can hide. We might even steer right into trouble. That's when we need to stop and let God be the driver. Hand out the stop signs.

On the stop signs write things you do or how you feel when you need to stop and let God be your driver. (Anger, twirling hair, crying, sleeping a lot, and so on.) Add the stop signs to the board. **No matter how we feel or what we do, we can be honking sure that God is the driver of our lives.**

Ask a volunteer to read Psalm 25:5. **When you feel out of control, hang on tight to the promises God gives in the Bible.** Hand out the photocopied Bibles. **Write down a promise in the Bible that lets you know that God is in control.** Some kids might like to copy Psalm 25:5. Attach Bibles with pushpins in different locations on the map. Then give the kids long pieces of yarn. Have each child attach a piece of yarn to a favorite promise and then to another promise and so on for a personal path or road map of hope.

- What will you remember the next time that you feel out of control?
- Who is always with you in your "life car" no matter what?
- Point to your favorite promise of hope from God.

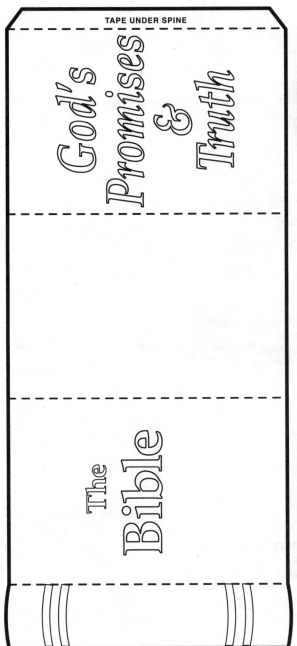

TAPE UNDER SPINE

God's Promises & Truth

The Bible

Out of Control!

STOP!
Let God Do the Driving.

Conquer the Mountain!

Bible Verse
Hebrews 10:36

You need to persevere so that when you have done the will of God, you will receive what he has promised.

Godprint
perseverance

As kids get older, the challenges get tougher! Kids will be tempted to give up, rather than stay with the hard tasks. By relying on God's strength, they can keep doing what he wants them to do.

Purpose

AS KIDS "CLIMB" THE MOUNTAIN AND OVERCOME VARIOUS OBSTACLES, THEY LEARN THAT GOD GIVES THE STRENGTH WE NEED TO COMPLETE HARD TASKS.

Get List

- Chicken wire
- Heavy-duty stapler and staples
- Double-sided tape
- Bulletin board paper in various colors
- Buttons
- Round wooden beads
- Chenille wires
- Permanent markers
- Scissors
- Hot glue gun and glue sticks
- Newspapers
- Craft sticks
- Construction paper
- Art tissue in various colors
- Small plastic wild animals
- Cotton balls or fiber-fill
- Gray and yellow tempera paints
- White glue
- Reproduce page 23

Construction Site: Make a three-dimensional mountain with roadblocks. Kids will add people.

1 Cover the bulletin board with blue paper.

2 Create the mountain using chicken wire stapled carefully to the bulletin board. If you're creating the bulletin board on a cinderblock wall, you can use hot glue to attach the wire. Angle the mountain so the low point is on the bottom left corner, climaxing at the peak in the top right corner. Make the chicken wire bow out, creating the 3-D effect. Stuff the wire with newspaper to give it support.

3 Use tape or hot glue to attach the wrinkled, brown and gray tissue paper onto the chicken wire. Use multiple layers to create a more colorful look as well as to give strength to the mountain.

4 Create a path by taping or gluing tan construction paper strips from the low point of the mountain to its peak. The path should run along the top of the mountain.

5 Crumple balls of tissue paper to create boulders. Tape or glue to the mountain. Add one or two boulders to the path.

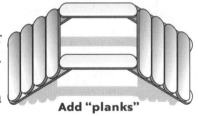
Add "planks"

6 Glue small plastic wild animals (such as a mountain lion or a bear) onto the path.

7 Create a craft stick bridge to cross a "valley" in the mountain. The bridge should be incomplete or should have a large hole in it to make it appear dangerous to cross.

Add broken "planks"

8 Glue cotton balls or fiber-fill in the sky above the mountain to create clouds. Use gray markers or paint to create a few storm clouds. Make a sun from yellow construction paper or fiberfill painted yellow. Glue the sun so that it appears to peek over the mountain. Copy the "God's Promises" shape from page 23 onto yellow paper. Cut out and glue onto the sun.

9 Cut out construction paper letters to create the bulletin board's title. Glue or tape along the top of the bulletin board. Copy the Bible verse and Godprint onto brown or gray paper. Cut out and glue or tape onto the bottom of the mountain.

10 In class, have the kids make people out of chenille wires, buttons and wooden beads. Add these characters to the bulletin board by stapling the "arms" onto the bulletin board back or taping them onto the mountain. Add speech balloons if desired.

 **Bend chenille wire.**

 **Lace one button onto wire. Place bead on wire.**

 **Add 2 buttons. Knot another chenille wire on for arms.**

 **Add more buttons. Twist chenille wires to secure. Spread out the "legs."**

Mini Lesson

Sometimes we have to do things that are very hard for us to do. **What are some hard things you've had to do?** Invite the kids to share. *(Kids might say things such as, my parents' divorce; take a test in school; learn to ride a two-wheeler; study the Bible every day; climb a mountain.)* **Look at our cool bulletin board. What "hard things" do you see?** *(The path is really steep; there's a boulder in the way; the bridge is broken; there's a bear ready to eat me!)*

The mountains and obstacles on our board are like the hard times we have. Sometimes we feel like giving up, don't we? But God helps us keep on trying until we finish the hard thing. We can know that God will give us his strength to help us through hard times. Ask a volunteer to read Hebrews 10:36. **What kinds of things does God promise to us?** *(Eternal life through Jesus Christ; peace; rest; love.)*

Let's make some people to put on the mountain. Show the kids how to make the button people. **Where would you like to put your person on the bulletin board? What do you think your person might say about persevering?** If you choose, add speech balloons for each person.

Spin-Offs: Personalize this bulletin board for your church. Perhaps your church has a service project or a building project to accomplish. Place the "goal" over the sun. Instead of roadblocks, add intermediate goals to accomplish. Move one "button person" along the path to show how much has been accomplished. You can also adapt this bulletin board to use with the following stories:

- Joshua perseveres in obeying God and conquers Jericho (Joshua 6:1–20).
- Nehemiah rebuilds the wall despite obstacles (Nehemiah 6–8).
- Ruth keeps on believing God (Ruth 1:1–4:18).

In following weeks, discuss hard times the kids have experienced recently. Invite the kids to move their button people and add new speech balloons as appropriate.

You need to persevere so that when you have done the will of God, you will receive what He has promised

Hebrews 10:36

PERSEVERANCE

When things get hard, we can keep going because God gives us strength.

God's Promises

Beat the Heat with God

Bible Verse
James 5:13

Is any one of you
in trouble? He
should pray.

Godprint
loyalty

Growing kids face
growing pressures.
Loyalty to God, rooted
in love and commitment
to his ways, helps kids
do what they know is
right regardless of
pressures and threats.

Purpose

BEING LOYAL TO GOD HELPS US FACE ALL OF LIFE'S CIRCUMSTANCES
AND CHALLENGES. KIDS WILL RECOGNIZE TROUBLES, CHALLENGES OR
HEATED SITUATIONS AND WILL DEVELOP "BUCKETS" FULL OF WAYS TO
PRAY AND REMAIN LOYAL TO GOD.

Get List

- Colored bulletin board paper
- Blue construction paper
- Large box
- Red tissue paper
- Glue gun and glue sticks
- Fan
- Orange streamers
- Small table
- Small nails
- Clear tape
- Scissors
- Foil
- Reproduce page 27
- *Optional: graham crackers*

Construction Site: Use a box to make a fiery furnace with flames that will jump up when the fan is turned on.

1 Line the inside of a large empty box with aluminum foil and glue the foil in place.

2 Tape the top and bottom of the box shut. Turn the box upside down. At the center of the bottom of the box, cut a 3" x 8" rectangle.

3 Cut streamers into 5–7" lengths, then cut them in half lengthwise. Tape the ends of the streamers around the edge of the rectangular opening on the bottom, overlapping about one inch on the outside and letting the rest of the streamer fall inside the box.

4 Turn the box right side up. Cut a large arch opening on one side of the box to view the flames inside the furnace. Wrap the box with colored bulletin board paper. Hot glue rectangular graham cracker sections onto the box or draw lines on the paper to look like bricks.

5 Cover the bulletin board with colored bulletin board paper. Place a small table just beneath the bulletin board. Attach the box to the bulletin board with small nails or hot glue so the arched opening faces out. The box should be high enough above the table so that a small fan can sit on the table and blow up through the box. Conceal the table with a drape of bulletin board paper taped from the bottom edges of the box down around the table.

6 Make the title, "Beat the Heat with God!" by cutting out letters from construction paper. Place the title at the top of the design, with flames of tissue paper behind the lettering.

Mini Lesson

Have you ever known someone who wanted you to go along with something and you knew it was going to be a bad situation—one where you could get in trouble? Sometimes situations get "hot" and we feel as if we're trapped in a fiery furnace. Let's think of times when troubles have flamed up for our friends or times when you've had to face the heat. Pass out copies of the flame. Have kids color in the flames, then draw or list heated situations they or others have faced. Tape the flames to the wall around the furnace.

Are you alone when you feel trapped in the fiery furnace? No! God is always with you. Although you can't see him, God is by your side even in times of trouble. He is with you in the furnace helping you endure the heat of life.

Spin-Offs: You can use the fiery furnace with the following Bible stories:

- Daniel and his friends face the heat (Daniel 3).
- Moses is fired up for God (Exodus 3).
- Elijah takes on the heat (1 Kings 18).

Turn on the fan and watch the flames jump up. Have the kids draw a picture of Jesus or God as a reminder of who is always with them in times of trouble. Glue the picture to the inside of the furnace. Make sure the fan is turned off and unplugged when you're not using it.

What do you do when you are facing the heat? Ask a volunteer to read James 5:13 from a Bible. **Praying is a great way to dump water on the fiery flames of trouble.**

• **What are other ways that you can show your loyalty to God and help yourself when you face the flames of trouble?**

• **Can you think of a Bible character who faced troubles or tough times? What did he or she do that was like dumping buckets of water on flames of trouble?**

Have the kids write these ideas on the water drops and color the drop blue. Assemble the photocopied buckets and tape them together. Kids can decorate the buckets. Then add the drops to the buckets of water and attach the buckets to the board.

Have the kids share all the things that they have added to the board. Emphasize how they can help each other be loyal to God during times of trouble.

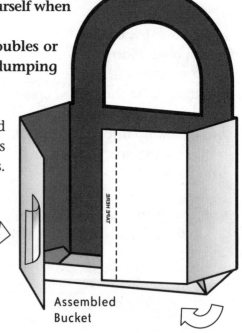

Assembled Bucket

• **What can you do when you face trouble?**
• **Tell me about someone you know who honored God in a time of trouble.**
• **Who is always with you in times of trouble?**

TAPE HERE

Creative Ceilings

&

Fantastic Floors

Chapter 2

"So many of these ideas are cool, but where do I get all this stuff?"

With interactive bulletin boards comes interactive hunting and seeking. You'll be able to gather most of the items that you'll need for these bulletin boards just by keeping your eyes open in the places you normally go. But a few wild and crazy items, like a steering wheel, may be harder to snag. If you're willing to invest the time and in most cases just a little money, there are ways to find these "off the wall" items.

- **Garage sales and junk yards.** Another person's junk may be just what you're looking for. Enjoy the look of surprise on your neighbor's face as you snatch up your bargain.

- **Ask and ye shall receive.** Many chain stores, grocery stores, fast food restaurants and hardware stores will donate items when they know you're from a church, school or non-profit organization. In some cases this may require a simple letter of request to the store manager.

- **Thrift stores.** Check out the thrift stores in your area. They'll have an amazing amount of stuff to hunt through.

- **Borrow from your congregation.** You'll be amazed at what other people have lying around at home or at work. A simple flyer with the items that you're looking for may be all the advertising you need.

Think *Safety*!

With interactive bulletin boards, think beyond the boards. Sometimes an ounce of prevention is invaluable. Eye-, hand- and head-catching items draw lots of attention. Remember safety, especially in a hallway. There's a chance that a tall person or two might bonk their heads on something hung in the center. Hanging items on the outer edge of the hallway may be less annoying. Also make sure you keep the walking areas wheelchair accessible. Ask yourself, "Are kids going to be tempted to jump through the hallway and bat at something hanging from the ceiling? The answer is, "Of course!" So be prepared to handle these issues beforehand.

Thinking about potential problems can help you prepare proactive responses. Redirect kids by offering suggestions for what they can do with the bulletin board. "I see you like our bulletin board. We're learning about friendship; would you like to add a friendship tea-bag to the board?"

Frequently, teachers do something in a classroom that's fun and inviting to kids—then back pedal and make rules once they see kids' creativity running awry. Define boundaries and set rules for the kids before they break them. But the best way to help kids respect the board is to let them invest in creating it. Enthusiastic learning will overcome the need for constant discipline.

Bee Attitudes

Bible Verse
Colossians 3:12

Therefore, as God's chosen people, holy and dearly loved, clothe yourselves with compassion, kindness, humility, gentleness and patience.

Godprint
humility

Kids want the first turn, the first snack, the first toy! Christ gives a different example—humility. He chose to give up what was rightfully his so we could have a relationship with God. Help the children bee-come humble as they learn to put the interests of others ahead of their own as Christ humbled himself for us.

Purpose
THE KIDS WILL "BEE" ACTIVELY INVOLVED IN LEARNING WHAT IT TAKES TO "BEE" HUMBLE.

Get List

- Egg cartons
- One hole punch
- Yarn
- Blue, brown bulletin board paper
- Chicken wire
- Artificial tree
- Construction paper
- Bibles
- Markers
- Tape
- Scissors
- Chenille wire
- Blankets
- Reproduce page 33

Construction Site: Build a hillside and beehive, then add an artificial tree.

1 Cover the bulletin board with blue bulletin board paper to create the sky. Use construction paper to make the title: "Bee-attitudes: Climb into a Humili-tree!" and attach to the bulletin board.

2 Make hills from the floor up to the bulletin board; the board becomes the sky background. Bend the chicken wire so that it takes the shape of hills, then cover the wire with brown bulletin board paper. Place the artificial tree off to one side of the bulletin board.

3 Cut the tops off the egg cartons and keep the bottoms with the egg cups. You might wish to have the kids help you construct this beehive by punching holes on the sides of the cartons and using yarn to tie them together snugly to form a hive. Hang the beehive from the ceiling, in front of bulletin board and near the tree. Make sure it's within the kids' reach.

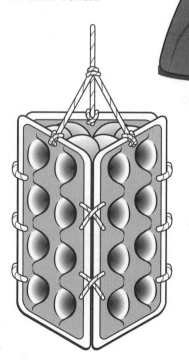

Mini Lesson

To set the stage, spread a blanket on the floor near the bulletin board. Invite the kids to join you on the blanket. **One day Jesus was speaking to a large group of people by the sea of Galilee. It may have been on a gently sloping hillside like the one here.** Point to the bulletin board. **Here, Jesus made a declaration of bee-lessings that we call the Beatitudes. We're going to call them *bee*-attitudes. Let's read them together.** Have the kids open their Bibles to Matthew 5:3–12 and read aloud.

Spin-Offs: You can use this bulletin board to talk about humility with these Bible stories:

• Jesus washes his disciples' feet (John 13).
• Daniel doesn't fight back, but shows humility (Daniel 6).

• **What are some of the attitudes Jesus talked about that day on the hill?** *(Meekness, righteousness, mercy, purity in heart, peacemaker.)*
• **What do you think Jesus was trying to teach?**

Now ask a volunteer to read Colossians 3:12.

• **How do the words in this verse remind you of what Jesus said in Matthew?**
• **A humble person will have compassion, kindness and patience. Tell about a humble person you know.**

You can use these activities as separate centers or introduce them one week at time. **Let's do some activities to help us learn about the bee-attitudes and how they can help us with our attitudes and help us to demonstrate humility.**

• **"Bee" right on target as you make bees that can attach to our beehive.** Have the kids color and decorate the bees from the reproducible page. **On the bees write ways to bee-have. Use the bee-atitudes in your Bible to help you come up with some ideas.** Attach the bees to the beehive or the bulletin board.

• **Add color to your life as you create flowers to add to our hillside.** Kids can use the reproducible flower as a pattern to make their own flowers out of construction paper and chenille wire. Or they can color the flower reproducible and tape it on a chenille wire to make a flower. **Write on the flowers a bee-attitude in your own words and then tell what you think it means.** Attach the flowers to the hillside or the bulletin board.

• **Don't be "leafed" out! Here are some leaves that you can hang on our humilitree.** Have the kids color and decorate the leaves. **Write the names of people you know who have shown humility. Then write down ways they have shown humility. Add more leaves with examples from your own life.**

Flower petals and leaves to attach to a chenille wire stem.

Times of Refreshing

Bible Verse
Acts 3:19

Repent, then, and turn to God, so that your sins may be wiped out, that times of refreshing may come from the Lord.

Godprint
repentance

As kids mature, they're more able to control their impulses and make intentional choices. Repentance is a choice to turn away from sin and selfishness and move toward God. God then blesses us with a refreshing freedom in his forgiveness and love.

Purpose

KIDS WILL EXPERIENCE A "QUIET MOMENT" WITH JESUS AT JACOB'S WELL. AFTER A TIME OF REFLECTION AND PRAYER, INVITE THEM TO WRITE A POSITIVE AFFIRMATION ON A PAPER, CRUMPLE IT UP AND TOSS IT INTO THE WELL AS THEY GO FORWARD FORGIVEN AND REFRESHED.

Get List

- Bulletin board paper
- Construction paper
- Art tissue paper
- Blue cellophane
- Tape
- Glue sticks
- Rubber cement
- Stapler
- Markers, crayons or paints
- Brown paper
- Garden bench or row of chairs
- Cereal boxes, garden edging stones or half a pickling barrel
- Bucket with rope
- Blue paper squares
- Pencils
- Oatmeal tubs
- Reproduce page 37
- *Optional: sand, plastic sheeting, 2x2 boards, bark pieces, dried leaves or moss, other 3-D decorations, opaque or overhead projector*

Construction Site: Make a "Jacob's Well." Kids will add prayers and Bible promises.

1 Measure the portion of the wall you plan to use with bulletin board paper. Using markers, crayons, paint or another medium, draw a peaceful looking mural to fit. In the background, create a path leading to a city. Attach the paper to the wall.

2 Add various three-dimensional items to the foreground portion of the mural to create interest. Cut oatmeal tubs in half and cover them with brown construction paper to make tree trunks. Crumpled green tissue paper becomes the trees' leaves or bushes. Glue small twigs onto the mural to add depth and texture. Glue pieces of bark to the mural to create a tree stump. Use craft sticks to create the city wall in the background.

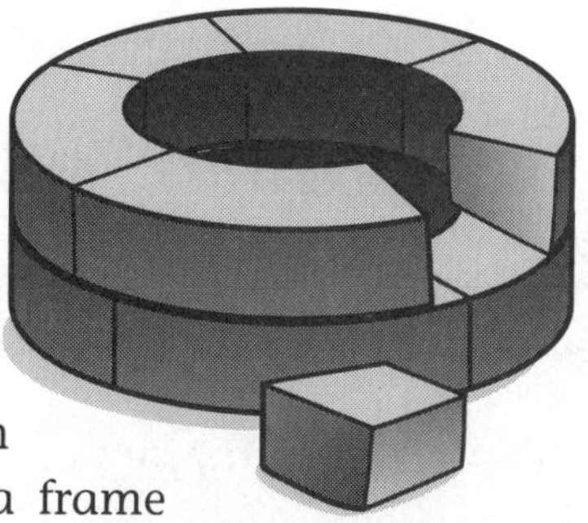

3 On the floor, create a sandy ground. You can staple plastic sheeting to a frame of 2′ x 2′ boards to create a shallow, lipped area for sand. If you'd rather not use real sand, create a sand-like floor by gluing sand onto brown bulletin board paper, or just use plain brown paper crumpled and taped to the floor.

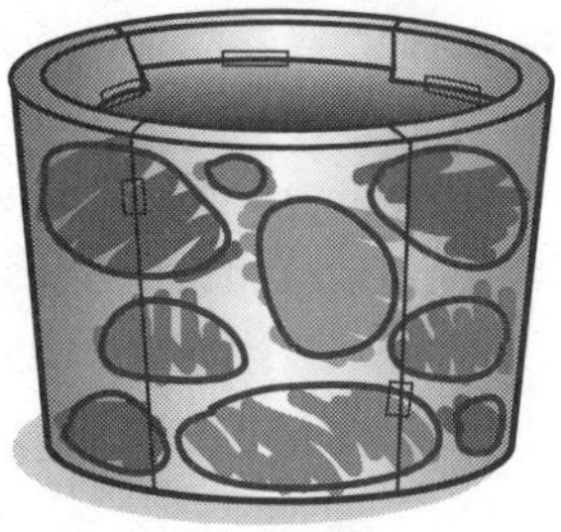

4 On the "sandy" floor, position the top portion of a well. Make a small circular "well." You can make "stones" by covering cereal boxes, or use real garden edging stones or half of a pickling barrel. Place crumpled blue cellophane into the well to represent water.

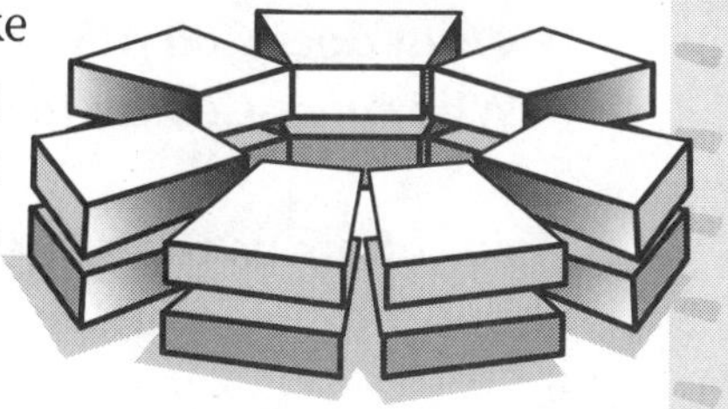

5 Beside the well, place a bucket with a rope tied to it and a garden bench or row of chairs to sit on. Place pencils and squares of blue paper inside the bucket.

6 Add the "Welcome to Jacob's Well" sign (see page 37) to the mural near the well. Place the "Acts 3:19" sign near the bench. Enlarge the images if you prefer.

Mini Lesson

- Can you think of somebody you know who dresses differently than you?
- How about somebody who moved here from another country or state?
- Do you know anyone who believes something different than what you believe?

Sometimes people who are not the same have trouble getting along. The Bible tells us about a time when Jesus met someone who was different, but he didn't have any trouble getting along.

Jesus and his friends were Jewish. While traveling one day, they stopped at a well. This well was in a place called Samaria. Samaritans lived there, and the Jewish people didn't like the Samaritans. A Samaritan woman came to the well for some water and Jesus asked her for a drink. She was surprised that Jesus spoke to her, because he was a Jew and she was a Samaritan. Then Jesus told her that he was the Living Water. He said, "Everyone who drinks this water will be thirsty again, but whoever drinks the water I give him will never thirst. Indeed, the water I give him will become in him a spring of water welling up to eternal life" (John 4:13). If you'd like, you can include more details from the story in John 4.

Spin-Offs: Use this interactive bulletin board to go along with a sermon about the Samaritan woman at Jacob's Well. Or, place pre-written affirmations or Bible promises into the well for people to pull out and keep as inspiration or encouragement. Hide story parts among the 3-D decorations of the mural to find and read to review the story. You can also adapt the well to use with these stories:

- God gives a bride for Isaac (Genesis 24).
- Joseph's brothers throw him in a cistern (Genesis 37).

Jesus took the time to speak with the woman at the well that day. The woman took the time to listen to Jesus. Because she listened, she believed that Jesus was truly the Messiah. She repented of her old way of life. The living water that Jesus talked about was a refreshing new life. Ask a volunteer to read Acts 3:19.

- **What does God ask us to do?** *(Turn from sin, repent.)*
- **What does God do for us?** *(Forgives us. Brings a time of refreshing.)*

Jesus offers us the same refreshing, living water and everlasting life that he offered the Samaritan woman. Show the bulletin board and the bucket of blue paper.

Let's each take some quiet time to talk with Jesus and to think about our lives, about our sins and about Jesus' love for us. When you feel ready, come to the bench and take a paper from the bucket. You can write a prayer or a reminder that Jesus loves you and forgives you. Then crumple up the note and throw it in the well. When we see the well full of water notes, we'll all remember that when we repent, God forgives us and refreshes our hearts! Older kids can help younger ones write notes or instruct them to draw a picture to place in the well.

Welcome to Jacob's Well

Repent, then, and turn to God, so that your sins may be wiped out, that times of refreshing may come from the Lord.

Acts: 3-19

Have a Ball Being Fair to Others

Bible Verse

Luke 6:31

Do to others as you would have them do to you.

Godprint

fairness

Kids let you know when something is not fair to them! But they can also recognize when they're not being fair to others. Help kids learn to treat others in an honest, equitable way, without selfishness, because God is just.

Purpose

KIDS WILL HAVE A BALL SCORING POINTS BY BEING FAIR TO OTHERS. THEY'LL LEARN ABOUT DIFFERENT WAYS TO PUT OTHERS FIRST AND HOW TO SHOW LOVE AND KINDNESS TO FAMILY AND FRIENDS.

Get List

- Colored bulletin board paper
- Construction paper
- Hula-hoop®
- Rope
- Orange, white and yellow balloons
- Large garbage bag
- Colored electrical tape
- Black permanent marker
- Large box
- String
- Green shower curtain or plastic tablecloth
- Duct tape
- Chenille wires
- 3 shoe boxes
- Wrapping paper
- Table tennis balls
- Spoons
- Cardboard
- Brown paper
- Straws
- Tape
- Newspaper
- Reproduce page 41
- *Optional: soccer goal*

Construction Site: Use floor and ceiling space to turn a section of your classroom into a stadium of sporting events.

1 Cover the bulletin board with colored bulletin board paper. Use construction paper to make the letters for the title, "Have a Ball Being Fair to Others." Tape the letters to the board. Add magazine pictures of sports stars to the bulletin board. Kids will add other stick-on items. Leave one corner covered only with brown paper and label it "Penalty Box."

2 To create the basketball court, tie two ropes at the top of a Hula-hoop®, 10 inches apart. Use the ropes to hang the Hula-hoop from the ceiling. Below the Hula-hoop mark four-foot by four-foot box on the floor with the colored electrical tape. Blow up several orange balloons. Use a black permanent marker to draw lines on the balloons to make them resemble basketballs. Store the balloon basketballs in a large garbage bag.

3 To create a soccer goal, use a large box. Cut an opening on the side of the box as large as you can make it. If you have a real soccer goal, use that! Blow up several white balloons and use the marker to draw lines on the balloons to make them resemble soccer balls. Tie three-foot pieces of string to the balloon soccer balls.

4 To make a football field, cut a six-foot by four-foot strip of green shower curtain or plastic tablecloth. Use a marker to draw lines on the football field. Duct tape the field to the floor. Bend chenille wires into goal posts and tape to each end of the football field. Set the paper footballs from page 41 near the football field.

5 To create a miniature golf course, use three shoe boxes. Wrap each box in colorful paper. Cut a different sized "mouse hole" in each box on one side, at the edge where the box meets the floor. Use duct tape to tape the boxes to the floor. Use electrical tape to mark a putting line on the floor up to 3' away from each box. Set the reproducible flags from page 41 and the straws near the golf center.

Mini Lesson

You can use these sporting events as separate interactive centers that teach the kids how to be fair and kind to others. You might prefer to introduce one each week. When kids complete score cards, they can take them home.

• **Tell me about a time when someone wasn't fair to you.**
• **What's the hardest thing about being fair?**

Spin-Offs: You can also talk about fairness and kindness with these stories:
• The Good Samaritan treats his enemy with kindness (Luke 10).
• Zacchaeus feels the pain of not being kind and learns to treat others fairly and with kindness (Luke 19).
• David could have gotten "even" with Saul, but treats him kindly (1 Samuel 24).

Ask a volunteer to read Luke 6:31. **Jesus wants us to be kind and fair to others even when it might be hard. Let's have a ball discovering ways to treat others in kind and fair ways as you would want them to treat you.** Explain the challenge of each of the centers.

Basketball: Take turns batting the balloon through the Hula-hoop®. With each hit, call out a way to be fair with friends. Point out the first section of the score card. It asks kids to write the name of one friend to be fair to this week.

Soccer: Take turns holding the ends of the strings and kicking the balloons through the goals. With each kick, shout out the Bible verse. On the score card, write what makes it hard to be fair or kind to others.

Football: Try to kick extra points by flicking wads of newspaper. With every flick that goes through the goal posts, call out a way to show kindness to a family member. Write ideas on the paper footballs and add them to the bulletin board. Write one way on the score card.

Golf: Use spoons for golf clubs and try to get the table tennis ball through a hole. With every "swing" call out something that you would like others to do for you. Then take a flag and write a positive way to treat others. Tape a straw to the flag and tape the flag to the board. Fill in the space on the score card.

Remember to be kind and fair as you play! At each sports center, check your score card and see how to score points. Write in answers to the questions. Point out the penalty box on the bulletin board. **Many times we blow it with our friends and family. We don't treat them kindly or fairly and we end up hurting their feelings. Tell about a time when this happened and write about what happened in the penalty box.**

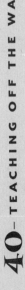

What would you like others to do for you?

ATTACH STRAW HERE

My Score Card: _____

Score 3 points by being fair to a friend. _____
_____
_____
_____

Kick in 1 point with what makes it hard to be kind or fair to others. _____
_____
_____

6 points plus 2 extra points when you think of ways to be kind to your family. _____
_____
_____

4 points if you can think of something you would like others to do 4 you.
_____
_____
_____

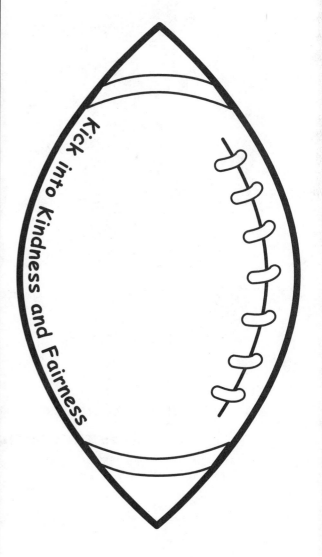

Kick into Kindness and Fairness

Keepin' Our Eyes on Jesus

Keeping Our Eyes on Jesus

Bible Verse

Hebrews 10:35

So do not throw away your confidence; it will be richly rewarded.

Godprint

confidence

When faced with new challenges, growing kids need confidence—a sense of security in their own abilities to accomplish a task because of faith and trust in God.

Purpose

KIDS WILL REFLECT ON THE HARD TIMES THEY FACE AND LEARN THAT GOD GIVES THE CONFIDENCE THEY NEED.

Get List

- 2" x 2" x 5' board
- 3' x 3' plywood
- 4" x 4" x 2" wood triangles
- Wood screws
- Screwdriver
- Wire coat hangers
- Large round balloon
- Newspaper
- Liquid starch
- Bowls
- Poster board
- Yarn
- Tempera paints
- Paintbrushes
- Glue
- Twine
- Small latex examination gloves
- Fiberfill
- Duct tape
- Strip of colorful fabric
- Hot-glue gun
- Blue and green cellophane
- Bulletin board paper
- Blue construction paper
- Markers or crayons
- Scissors
- Gray or silver spray paint
- Old sheet
- Reproduce the waves on page 45 to use as a pattern
- *Optional: Glitter, gel pens*

Construction Site: Make a sea background with a 3-D Jesus standing and reaching out. Kids will add waves of confidence to the sea.

1 Spray-paint an old white sheet or quilt batting to resemble storm clouds. When it's dry, attach the sheet to the ceiling in several places for a sky of storm clouds.

2 Securely cover an area of wall from floor to ceiling with blue bulletin board paper. Using bulletin board paper or construction paper, as well as markers or paint, create a background scene on the blue paper. You'll need a stormy sky, the shoreline of the lake (the blue paper is the lake), hills in the horizon and a partial view of a fishing boat. You may want to put a few dismayed disciples in the fishing boat as well.

3 Create a wooden stand for the "Jesus" figure you will create. Attach a 2" x 2" board onto a 3-foot square piece of plywood using four wooden triangles for support.

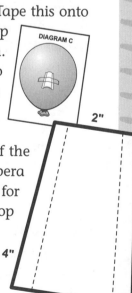

Wood Screws

2" x 2" x 5'

Plywood

4 Inflate a large round balloon for Jesus' head. Cut a 2" x 4" x 3" piece of poster board and fold the long edges as shown in the digram. Tape this onto the balloon to become the nose. Dip strips of newspaper into liquid starch. Use your index and middle fingers to squeeze excess starch off the strip, then apply the strip to the balloon. Cover the entire balloon with strips and let dry. You may need to repeat this process if the papier mâché is too thin. Use tempera paints to create Jesus' face. Glue on yarn for hair and beard. Hot-glue Jesus' head onto the top end of the wooden support.

DIAGRAM C

2"

4"

3"

5 Straighten two heavy wire clothes hangers. Wrap the ends around the 2" x 2" board and attach them with duct tape or staples. These become the supports for Jesus' arms. Bend the arms so that Jesus appears to be reaching out. Drape a length of colorful fabric or robe over the frame. If you like, you can wrap newspaper around the wires for some padding.

6 Stuff two examination gloves with fiberfill. Rubber band and tape the opening closed. Use twine and tape to secure the "hands" to the ends of Jesus' wire arms. Pull the robe's arms over the "wrists" to hide the tape and twine.

7 Place your finished Jesus in front of the bulletin board's background. Finish the bulletin board by crumpling blue and green cellophane to represent water. Tape the crumpled cellophane securely to the floor, surrounding Jesus and covering his unseen feet.

8 Write, "Keepin' Our Eyes on Jesus" on the poster board. Hang it with yarn from the "clouds" over Jesus' head.

Mini Lesson

• **How do you feel when you get caught in the middle of a storm?**

Sometimes life feels like we're in the middle of a storm, and it's hard to see where we're going. Let's look at a Bible Story about someone feeling like that. In a Bible, find the story of Jesus and Peter walking on the water in Matthew 14:22–33. If kids are familiar with the story, let them tell you the details, or ask a volunteer to read it.

• **What amazing thing did Jesus do in this story?** *(Walked on the water.)*
• **What happened when Peter tried to walk on water?**
  (He could until he got scared and started to sink.)

When Peter got out of the boat, his eyes were fixed on Jesus. He was confident that Jesus would help him walk on water. Then he saw the wind and got scared. Without his confidence in Jesus, he started to sink. When we focus on Jesus and not the problems in our lives, Jesus gives us the confidence we need to get through stormy times. Invite the kids to share what they see on the bulletin board and wall display. Then ask a volunteer to read Hebrews 10:35.

• **What does this verse say that we should do with our confidence?** *(Hang on to it!)*

> **Spin-Offs:** Use the waves as an aid to prayer time from week to week. Write requests and answers to prayer and keep adding waves of confidence. You can also adapt this display to use with these stories:
>
> • Paul's confidence in God during a shipwreck (Acts 27)
> • Moses' confidence in God when crossing the Red Sea (Exodus 13–14)

Let's make "Waves of Confidence" to add to our bulletin board. They will help us to remember to keep our eyes on Jesus for confidence. Pass out copies of the wave (page 45). Show how to fold blue construction paper in half and trace the wave shape so that the top of the wave is on the fold of the paper. Cut out the waves, being careful not to cut the fold. Invite the kids to decorate the outsides. Inside, have them write or draw about a stormy time in their lives. Tape them onto the lake on the bulletin board.

FOLD

FOLD

Take a Hike!
(In Someone Else's Shoes)

Bible Verse
Ephesians 4:32

Be kind and compassionate to one another, forgiving each other, just as in Christ God forgave you.

Godprint
empathy

God wants us to show empathy towards others as Christ identified with our need and showed kindness, grace and empathy towards us. Help the kids express empathy by identifying with what another person is feeling and experiencing.

Purpose

A GREAT WAY TO SHOW COMPASSION AND FORGIVENESS TOWARD OTHERS IS TO "TAKE A HIKE" IN THEIR SHOES. KIDS WILL EXPERIENCE STANDING IN OTHER PEOPLE'S SHOES AND DO A LITTLE SOUL SEARCHING INTO THE THOUGHTS AND FEELINGS OF OTHERS.

Get List

- Large tree branch or branches
- Gallon-size plastic container
- Sand, cement mix or Plaster of Paris
- Colorful bulletin board paper
- Cotton balls
- Poster board
- Stapler
- Construction paper
- String
- Old shoes (one pair from each child)
- Old magazines
- Scissors
- Glue sticks
- Reproduce page 49.
- *Optional: artificial Christmas tree*

Construction Site: Make a mountain range scene and use a tree as part of the bulletin board.

1 Mix the cement or Plaster of Paris according to package directions. Pour it into the plastic container. Put the branches into the container and allow time to set. A bucket of samd will work also. Optional: use an artificial Christmas tree.

2 Cover the top of the bulletin board with blue bulletin board paper to create the sky. Then add brown paper for mountains. Now glue cotton balls to the top of the mountains to look like the peaks are covered with snow. Cover the bottomof the board with

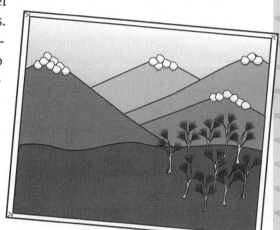

green paper. In the corner where you'll place the large tree, tape small branches so they look like a grove of trees in the landscape leading to the large tree.

3 Use poster board to make a hiking path coming out of the mountains towards the large tree. Cut the poster board into winding strips that are thicker at the bottom (closest to the tree) and thinner at the top (in the mountains) to give the illusion of distance. To give the path a three-dimensional effect, attach with staples as you bend the poster board into wavy sections. Near the path, add the title, "Take a Hike! (In Someone Else's Shoes)" cut from construction paper.

Mini Lesson

Imagine a small village at the base of a large mountain. When the village people have arguments, they go to see the Shoe Man. A shoe man, you say? Yes, a very wise man who lives at the edge of the town near a huge, very strange looking tree. Often the people who come to see the Shoe Man are angry, bitter and not very nice to each other. The Shoe Man always tells them to trade shoes with the other person. Then the Shoe Man sends them out on a hike together. When they return, their problems are always mysteriously solved. The Shoe Man takes their old shoes and sells them a new pair.

After they leave, the Shoe Man tosses their shoes into the huge tree. If the people ever return, the Shoe Man takes them to the tree and reminds them that it only takes a hike in another's shoes to learn more about each other. When you walk in someone else's shoes, you find out what the person is thinking and feeling. Then you are ready to show compassion and understanding.

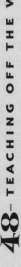

Spin-Offs: You can also use this bulletin board with these stories:
- Jesus forgives us (Mathew 18).
- Four men know how their friend feels (Mark 2).

- **What can we learn from the Shoe Man?**
- **Why would people's problems be solved when they returned from their hike?**

Ask a volunteer to read Ephesians 4:32.

- **What does this verse say God wants us to do?**
- **Why should we treat others this way?**

Knowing what another person is feeling can really help us understand that person in a different way. It is as though we are walking in their shoes. Having empathy towards another starts by understanding feelings. Let's think of some feeling words. Brainstorm "feeling words," then have the kids write feeling words on the photocopied shoe prints. Tape the shoe prints to the floor in a path around the room that leads to the bulletin board. Have the kids take a hike. As they step onto a "feeling word," have them come up with a scenario of what happened to make a person feel that way. Then have them say what they might do to help.

Let's see if we can take a hike in someone's shoes as we explore how others might feel. Have the kids cut out pictures of people from magazines and tape them to the paper shoes. On the other side of the shoe, ask them to write what they think happened to this person and how he or she might be feeling. Tuck the paper shoes into their old pair of shoes. Hang the shoes in the tree or attach a string to the paper shoes and hang from the ceiling. **On your hiking guide, write down the name of a person you have had a hard time getting along with lately. Write down how you might try to understand, show compassion or even forgive that person.**

My Hiking Guide: _____

Someone I'm having a hard time with.

What's the person's point of view?
_____
_____
_____

How might this person feel?

What will I do?
_____
_____
_____

Chapter 3

The Home Links bulletin boards help kids reach out to their families and to the community around them. Kids will have an opportunity to pray for each other, to instigate activities at home with their families and to participate in meaningful group service activities.

You can adapt the bulletin boards in this chapter for whole-church use. Put them up in a busy place in your church and invite everyone to participate in the activities. Use more than one board for the same theme so that everyone can get involved. Encourage parents, in particular, to pick up the "take home" part of each bulletin board and let their kids lead them through the activity.

Some of these boards display information that will change from week to week. Give kids ownership of the boards by involving them in putting it up and then making them responsible for weekly updates under supervision. Other bulletin boards in this chapter display ongoing projects or services or ask families to do something at home. You'll want to update these each week and allow plenty of time for families to make their contributions.

Enthusiasm is contagious! The kids will catch your enthusiasm and then pass it on to their families—and to the whole church! Almost every church has an "information" board. Make yours exciting and fun—something everyone wants to investigate every week.

Meeting Needs, Sharing Joy

Godprint

helpfulness

Helpfulness is giving aid to people simply because they need it. As we are helpful, we reflect the many ways God comes to our aid.

Purpose

KIDS WILL SEE THE MANY OPPORTUNITIES THEY HAVE TO SHARE GOD'S LOVE IN MEANINGFUL AND PRACTICAL WAYS IN THEIR OWN COMMUNITY.

Get List

- Vinyl shower curtain
- Permanent black marker
- Fun-edged scissors
- Construction paper
- Bulletin board paper
- Markers
- Rubber cement
- Double-sided tape
- Glue sticks
- Camera
- Lots of film!
- *Optional: scrapbook background papers, stickers, stamps and inkpads, die-cuts, a scrapbook "expert" from the congregation*

Construction Site: Create a giant scrapbook that your group can help use to plan service projects and celebrate helpfulness.

1 Before constructing your bulletin board, choose the community service projects your group will do. You can choose projects kids can do, or involve the whole church. Make arrangements with the community groups, pick up literature and take photos of the places your group will be visiting. Whatever age span you choose for the projects, make sure to have kids be responsible for updating the bulletin board.

2 Lay out a white- or cream-colored shower curtain. Use a yardstick and a permanent black marker to create a book-like appearance by drawing a dividing line down the center. Make the book look 3-D by drawing page edges along the sides and bottom. Secure the shower-curtain to a bulletin board or a wall.

3 Label the left-hand side of your scrapbook bulletin board "Community Needs." Use brightly colored construction paper letters or pre-cut lettering. You'll find some letter outlines to trace on page 55. Create a background for each letter by using contrasting colors and fun-edged scissors. Display the pamphlets from the various organizations promoting your projects. Create eye-catching labels for each pamphlet. Use the name of the establishment you will help, or the type of volunteering you'll do there. Create a project list for each organization, with dates, times and specific comments. For extra fun, make a background for each list that matches the pamphlet you have from that organizatin. background. Use rubber cement or double-sided tape to secure each to the shower curtain's left-hand side.

4 Label the right-hand side of your scrapbook bulletin board, "Ways We've Helped." Use brightly-colored construction paper letters or pre-cut lettering. Create a background for each letter using contrasting colors and fun-edged scissors. As kids or other members of the congregation carry out the projects, take lots of photos! Display the photos with captions and fun backgrounds. Add stickers and die-cuts to both sides of the bulletin board.

Ashton Villa Homes

- *Totally Tea!*
  March 2, 2-4pm
- *Day to Play!*
  April 4, 1-5pm
  Skits, songs, & games
- *Pets for People!*
  May 6, 1-5pm
  Bring pets of all sorts to share.

Daniel & Mrs. Isaac enjoy Michael's attention.

5 Let kids help update the board periodically. Create backgrounds for any thank-you cards your church receives and display them along with the photos.

Mini Lesson

• Tell me about the last time someone helped you.
• What about the last time you helped someone else?
> • Why is helping other people important to you?

Spin-Offs: Use this bulletin board to keep track of church-wide community service projects and let the kids make new additions. You can also adapt this bulletin board to use with these stories:

• The Good Samaritan helps a stranger (Luke 10:25–37)
• Lessons on the miracles of Jesus helping others.

The most important way that we can help someone is to know God. When you help someone, you show God's love. Sometimes we don't even have to say a word. We're going to choose some ways to help other people and celebrate along the way.

If you've chosen your service projects ahead of time, show the left side of your "scrapbook." You might prefer to involve kids in choosing projects and let them help you construct the scrapbook over a period of time. They can cut out letters and backgrounds. Older kids can help with writing lists and information.

Talk about how each of the projects that you've selected will help others. Then ask a volunteer to read Hebrews 6:10.

• How do we show love for God when we help others?
• How do you think God feels when we help others?
• What makes you want to help other people?
• What's your favorite way to help?

Ask a volunteer to read Matthew 23:11: "The greatest among you will be your servant." Ask someone else to read Mark 9:35: "If anyone wants to be first, he must be the very last, the servant of all."

• Where does Jesus say greatness comes from? *(Being a servant.)*

You probably noticed that the right side of the bulletin board isn't done. After we've helped people, we'll decorate this side with photographs of our projects, using thank-you cards that we may receive, or any other way you think would be nice.

Aa Bb Cc Dd Ee Ff Gg

Hh Ii Jj Kk Ll Mm Nn

Oo Pp Qq Rr Ss Tt Uu

Vv Ww Xx Yy Zz

Get a Bang Out of Life!

Get a **BANG** Out of
Life
Balloon-Busting Ways to
Tell Others "I Love You"!

And live a life of
love, just as Christ
loved us and gave
himself up for us as
a fragrant offering
and sacrifice to God.

Godprint
enthusiasm

Creating an
environment where
everyone can get a
bang out of life will
help kids develop a
glad spirit about the
purpose and work that
God gives them as
members of a family.

Purpose

**WE CAN HAVE A BLAST LEARNING TO LOVE OTHERS AS CHRIST LOVED
US. GIVE THE KIDS AND THEIR PARENTS OPPORTUNITIES TO SERVE, TO
BE KIND AND TO LOVE EACH OTHER.**

Get List

- Wrapping paper with balloons and confetti
- 50 uninflated balloons
- Construction paper
- Poster board
- Confetti, streamers, curling ribbon
- Push pins
- Hole punch
- Pens or markers
- Reproduce page 59

Construction Site:

Have the kids help you create this bulletin board by stuffing balloons with loving ideas and attaching the balloons to the board.

1 Cover the bulletin board with wrapping paper.

2 Use the construction paper to cut out the letters for the title: "Get a bang out of life! Balloon-busting ways to tell others, 'I love you!'"

3 Glue the letters to a sheet of poster board. Hang the poster board above the bulletin board and dangle streamers from it.

Mini Lesson

- Tell me what you know about your parents' jobs. Do they like their jobs?
- What kind of jobs do you do? Do you like the jobs that you do?

No matter where we go to work or school, God gave each of us one job to do. What do you think it is? Pause for answers, then ask a volunteer to read Ephesians 5:2.

- What is the job God gives each of us? *(Live a life of love.)*
- Who shows us how to do this job? *(Christ showed us by loving us.)*

Because he loved us, God gave us the greatest gift ever, his Son Jesus. He wants us to show others love too by living a life of love. And he wants us to do it gladly!

- How can we live a life of love?
- Is it hard or easy to be glad about living a life of love? Why?

One way we can gladly show others that we love them is by the things that we do. Let's really concentrate and think of some ways that we can show others we love them. Some ideas are: clean the car, clean my room, make a greetingcard, draw a picture, read to someone, give hugs, back rubs, paint fingernails, play a game, ride bikes. Hand out the photocopied "I love you" slips. Have the kids write one idea on each slip.

- How do you feel when you show love to someone else?
- What makes you glad about showing love to someone?

Hand out the reproduced firecrackers. Then pass out the balloons. You'll need enough completed "I love you" slips and enough firecrackers for each balloon to have one of each. If you stuff some extra balloons, parents will be able to participate later.

Now let's stuff an "I love you" slip in each balloon. Then blow up the balloon and tie the end of it. Next tie a ribbon to the balloon and attach your firecracker to end of the ribbon. Have the kids punch a hole in the firecracker where indicated. **Then I'll help you attach the balloon to the bulletin board.** Use pushpins to attach the tied end of the balloon to the bulletin board. If possible, prepare more balloons than you have kids so that some of them can remain on the board.

After all the balloons are attached to the board, congratulate the kids on their hard work. **Now here comes the fun part. I guarantee it will be a blast. Everyone will get to take one balloon home.** If you have enough balloons, when parents arrive, suggest they each grab a balloon as well. **When you get home pop the balloon. Then it's your turn to do what it says on the "I love you" slip for someone at home. Fill out the firecracker and tell us all about the bang you got out of sharing your love with others.** Bring the firecrackers back and we'll put them up on the bulletin board.

Have a blast showing one another your love!

Spin-Offs: This balloon-busting board could be used for giving or making gifts for the elderly. You can also use it for words that build each other up or for giving meaningful compliments. You can adapt the reproducible to use with these stories:

• David and Jonathan show friendship (1 Samuel 18:1–14).
• Jesus wants us to show honor to others (Luke 14:7–14).

I GOT A **BANG** OUT OF LIFE FROM:

IT WAS A **BLAST** BECAUSE:

XOXOXOXOXOXOXOXOXOXOXOXOXOXOXOX

I LOVE YOU

One way I can show love to others is to...

Prayerz and Prayz!

Bible Verse

Colossians 4:2

Devote yourselves to prayer, being watchful and thankful.

Godprint

prayerfulness

Is God always with us? Yes! Help kids to learn be mindful of the presence and power of God in all situations and to call on God because he hears and responds.

Purpose

KIDS WILL SHARE PRAYER REQUESTS WITH EACH OTHER AND USE PRAYER JOURNALS TO REMEMBER TO PRAY FOR EACH OTHER.

Get List

- Plastic strawberry baskets
- Art tissue paper
- Bulletin board paper
- Construction paper
- Shape scissors
- Stapler
- Tape
- Glue
- Markers or crayons
- Yarn
- Pushpins
- Pencils or pens
- Instant camera or pictures of students
- Hole punch
- Reproduce page 63
- *Optional: glitter, sequins, stickers, other decorative items, hot glue gun*

Construction Site: Create a class journal of prayerz and prayz. Kids will add pictures and baskets.

1 Cover the bulletin board with brightly colored paper.

2 Cut out letters from construction paper to create the following titles or signs:
- Prayerz 'n' Prayz!
- Let us pray for you!
- Let us rejoice with you!
- Prayz to Share!
- Prayerz Slips
- Prayz Slips
- The name of your class or group
- Devote yourselves to prayer, being watchful and thankful (Colossians 4:2).

Staple the title along the top of the bulletin board. Staple the Bible verse along the bottom. Place the Prayerz Slips basket and Prayz Slips basket and signs in the lower right-hand corner of the bulletin board. Create an area for "Prayzez to Share!" above the baskets.

3 Set out baskets, construction paper weaving strips and decorating supplies for kids to use.

4 Cut strips of art tissue or construction paper to fit the height of the spaces in the basket walls. If you're using construction paper, kids may want to decorate it with markers or crayons. Weave the strips of paper through two strawberry baskets to cover all sides as well as the bottom. Attach the two baskets to the bulletin board in the lower right hand corner. These will hold the Prayer and Prayz slips.

5 Ask kids to bring photographs of themselves from home or have an instant camera available.

Mini Lesson

Begin by having kids make their baskets. They can weave construction paper strips into the baskets and decorate as freely as they wish. Then have them make name tags to tack below their baskets on the board. If you have scissors with a fun-shaped edge, kids will enjoy making decorative edges on their tags.

Next, have kids make backgrounds or frames for their photos. Attach the photos to the bulletin board with staples. Next to each photo, place each child's basket with the name tag underneath.

Spin-Offs: Use the baskets, pictures and nameplates idea to show off lightweight creations that the kids make. You can also adapt this board to use with these stories:

• Jesus teaches his disciples to pray (Matthew 6:5–13).
• The believers pray for Peter's release from prison (Acts 12:5–17).

• **What do you think we're going to do with these photos and baskets?** *(Let kids speculate. Some will figure out the theme from the title on the board.)*
• **Tell me about times when you pray.**

Ask a volunteer to read Colossians 4:2.

• **What does it mean to be "devoted" to something?**
• **How can we show that we're devoted to prayer?**

We're going to show that we're devoted to praying for each other. You can take a prayer slip or a prayz slip from the baskets. Use different colored paper for the Prayerz and Prayz slips for easy sorting. **You can write a prayer request or a note praising God on your slip of paper. Then put it in someone else's basket. Do as many as you want to do.**

Allow some time for kids to fill out slips and put them in baskets. Make sure that everyone's basket gets some slips. Write some extras if you need to.

Do we only want to pray for each other while we're here? No! We want to be devoted to prayer. So let's make a prayer journal. Let kids decorate two pieces of construction paper for their prayer journal covers. Distribute copies of page 63. Punch a hole in the top left-hand corner of each journal page and cover. Add three prayer journal pages and bind the journal together with yarn.

When you get a prayer request in your basket, write that information down in your Prayer 'n' Prayz journal. Pass the slip on to someone else's basket. Then pray for that request as often as you remember. Assure the kids that you can make more copies of the journal pages when they need them.

If you have an answer to prayer, you can write a note to put on the Prayzes to Share part of our board. That way everyone can rejoice together in God's answer to prayer.

date: _____   date: _____
_____   _____
_____   _____
_____   _____
_____   _____

date: _____
_____
_____
date: _____
_____
_____

DATE: _____
_____
_____
DATE: _____
_____
_____

DATE: _____
_____
_____
_____
_____   DATE:

My Prayerz 'n' Prayz Journal page _____

Kicking into Family Goals

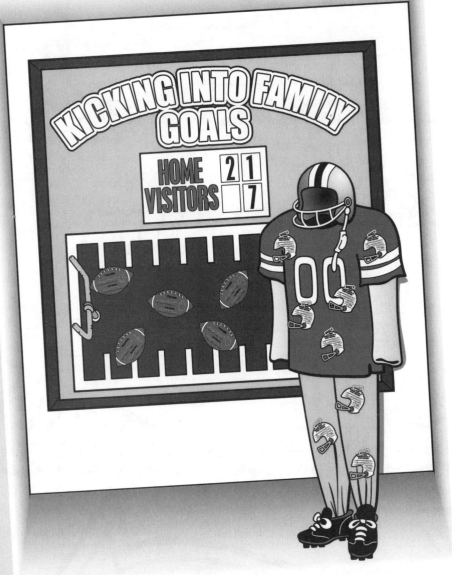

Bible Verse

Proverbs 14:22

But those who plan what is good find love and faithfulness.

Godprint

purposefulness

Help kids understand that God has a winning game plan and purpose for their lives, which includes being a terrific team member on their family team.

Purpose

KIDS WILL LEARN THAT A GOOD FAMILY TEAMMATE WILL USE DEFENSIVE STRATEGIES TO PROTECT THEIR FAMILIES, AND OFFENSIVE STRATEGIES TO HELP SCORE POINTS WITH EACH OTHER FOR MORE TRUSTING RELATIONSHIPS.

Get List

- Football gear: helmet, shoulder pads, pants, jersey
- Green bulletin board paper
- Poster board
- Push pins or small nails
- Yellow chenille wire
- Plasti-Tak®
- Reproduce page 67

Construction Site:
If your bulletin board is large enough attach football gear to one side and make a small football field on the other side. If you have a smaller board, stuff a football player wearing the gear and place him in a chair in front of the bulletin board.

1 Cover the bulletin board with the green bulletin board paper. Use a poster board to make a scoreboard with the title "Kicking into Family Goals."

2 On one side of the bulletin board, attach the helmet, shoulder pads, jersey and pants. You can pull the jersey over the shoulder pads. Use push pins or small nails to attach or hang these items on the board.

3 On the other half of the bulletin board, draw a football field. Make a rectangle 2' x 3'. Mark off "yards" on the field. Use the chenille wire to make goal posts and tape to them each end of the field.

Mini Lesson

How is a family like a football team? Give the kids time to discuss. Families are like football teams in many ways. Let's talk about one of them.

Many factors help make a football team successful, but one of the real biggies is the game plans that the coach and team follow. Defensive plans help protect the home team from the opponents. Offensive plans help the home team score points and win the game! Our families need good plans

too. Ask a volunteer to read the second part of Proverbs 14:22 from a Bible: "...those who plan what is good find love and faithfulness."

• What happens when we have a good plan?
• What positive things can happen in your family with a good plan?

God wants our homes and families to be filled with love and faithfulness. A good defensive plan helps the family stick together. A good offensive plan helps the family score points for great relationships.

Hand out the photocopied helmets.

• **What are some things that you think families can do to help each other stick together?** *(Spend time with each other, play together, communicate, eat together, share.)*

Give the kids time to brainstorm. Then have them write their answers on the helmets. Have the kids tape the helmets to any part of the football equipment. **These are all great things that will help a family be a winning team.**

Spin-Offs: Use a board like this one to help kids explore setting personal goals or classroom goals. You can also adapt this idea to use with these stories:

• Nehemiah works toward the goal of rebuilding the wall (Nehemiah 1–8).
• Noah follows God's good plan (Genesis 6–9).

Hand out the footballs. **Now it's time to come up with a great name for your winning team. Put your family team name on a football. You can also add your own team logo if you wish.** Use the Plasti-Tak® to put the footballs on the center of the football field.

Now here's the plan. Hand out the "Kicking Into Family Goals" sheet. **Start by putting your family team name on the sheet. You'll take this home and have your family help you fill it out. Your family will come up with a plan for one thing to do together this week that you don't usually do. This could be to play a game, read a book together, go for a walk, or a bike ride. Then bring your sheet back the next time you come. Every time your family completes its goal you get to move your football one line closer to the goalpost on the field. Take another goal sheet and keep going!**

• What are some things that make a family successful?
• What can you do to help your family team?
• Show me a cheer for your family team.

ONE THING FAMILIES CAN DO TO STICK TOGETHER:

_____
_____
_____
_____
_____

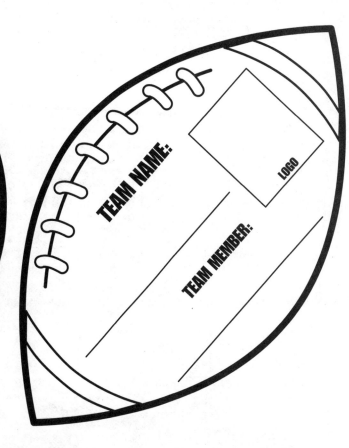

TEAM NAME:

LOGO

TEAM MEMBER:

KICKING INTO FAMILY
GOALS

FAMILY TEAM NAME:

TEAM MEMBERS:

THIS WEEK, THIS IS WHAT WE'LL DO TOGETHER AS A TEAM:

Tea of Truth

Bible Verse
2 John 1:4

It has given me great joy to find some of your children walking in the truth, just as the Father commanded us.

Godprint
honesty

As children's consciences develop, so does their sense of honesty. They realize that they can deceive by what they say as well as what they don't say, by what they do and by what they don't do. God wants us to reflect his truthfulness.

Purpose

KIDS—AND THEIR FAMILIES, IF YOU'D LIKE—WILL DECIDE THE HONEST ACTION TO TAKE IN A VARIETY OF SITUATIONS.

Get List

- Paper or Styrofoam® cups
- Small paper plates
- Markers or crayons
- Rubber cement or hot-glue gun
- Stapler
- Tape
- Bulletin board paper
- Construction paper or poster board
- Scissors
- Tea bags with tags
- Plastic spoons
- Reproduce page 71
- *Optional: small wicker basket, individually wrapped mints, Victorian wallpaper scraps, stickers, glitter glue, other decorative items*

Construction Site: Prepare a "table" and kids will help decorate and add cup-and-saucer sets with spoons and teabags.

1 Cover the bulletin board with pastel-colored bulletin board paper. You may also use scrap wallpaper in a simple Victorian style. Create a border using a compatible color. See the border samples on page 71.

2 Use the lettering samples on page 71 and create the title, "Tea of Truth," and staple it along the top of the bulletin board.

3 Using the pattern (see page 71) let each child make a situation card. Choose conflict situations that will be common experiences for the kids in your group.(See the mini lesson for examples.) Tape each card to the hand of a plastic spoon.

4 Create three teabag tags for each situation card, using the pattern on page 71. Each tag will offer a response to the conflict (at least one response should be based on truth and honesty). Tape or glue the tags over the original teabag tags.

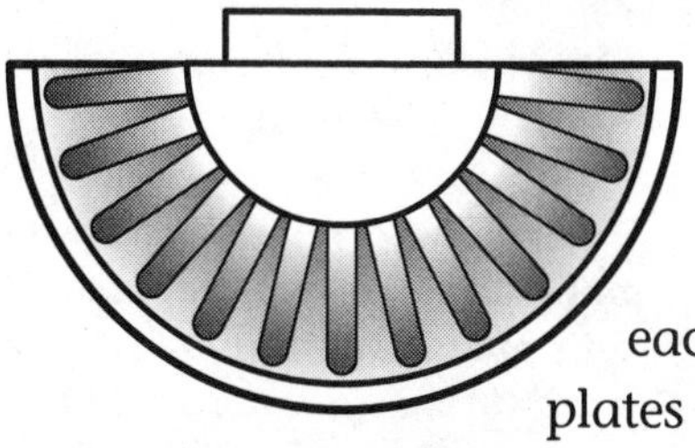

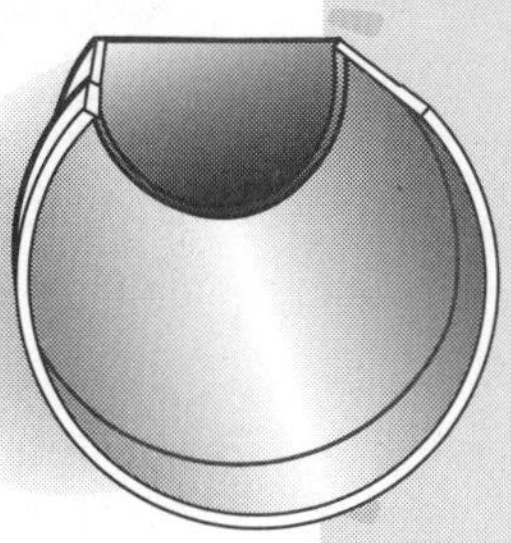

5 Cut away one-quarter of a Styrofoam® or paper cup, lengthwize. Prepare enough for each child (or family) to have one cup. Cut paper plates in half, then trim each half to leave a 1-inch tab across the center (see the illustration at left). Each child or family will need one half-plate to form the saucer for his or her tea set.

6 Let the kids decorate their cup-and-saucer sets. When they're dry, rubber cement the decorated cup to the saucer, then staple or tape the saucer's tab onto the bulletin board. (A bit of rubber cement on the cup's edges will affix the tea set even more firmly to the board.) Place one spoon with a situation card in each cup. Place the three matching teabags with tags onto the saucer so the tags hang down.

3-D ADVENTURES —

69

Mini Lesson

This is a great bulletin board to create with entire families working together. However, the children in your class can do it just as well.

- **What does the word "honest" mean to you?**
- **When might it be hard for someone to be honest?**

To be honest means that we are truthful with our words and our actions. Being honest isn't always an easy thing to do. Ask a volunteer to read 2 John 1:4.

- **What does it mean to "walk in the truth"?**
- **Why should we walk in truth?** *(The Father commanded it.)*
- **According to this verse, what reaction could others have when we walk in the truth?** *(Joy.)*

The greatest truth of all is that God sent his Son for us so that we can live the way God wants us to live—in truth. We're going to create a bulletin board that will help us think about honest words and honest actions that show we walk in the truth. Make sure every child has a "cup and saucer" to decorate. Help them attach the tea sets to the bulletin board.

Now for the "Tea of Truth." I'm going to give you a spoon with a situation on the handle, and three tea bags. I want you to read the situation on the spoon, and write three different things you might do in that situation. You may have some tricky answers, but make sure that one of your ideas is an honest answer. Pass out the spoons, tea bags and tags. Older kids can help younger kids write. When kids finish the tea tags, have them place a spoon and the three tea bags that go with it on a saucer on the board.

When everyone's finished, invite kids to choose someone else's tea set, read the spoon and the three tags and tell which response they think is the honest one and why. Place the "honest" tea bag in the cup.

Spin-Offs: Add a lightweight wicker basket of after-dinner mints to the board. Each child or family who completes the activity can enjoy a mint. Use the teabag activity for any sort of "matching" activity, such as matching a person's name from the church with the ministry the person helps with. You can also adapt this board to use with these Bible stories:

- Zacchaeus learns from Jesus to be honest (Luke 19)
- Peter wishes he had chosen honesty (Mark 14)

Sample situations and responses:

1. You saw a cookie on a plate and ate it. Later, your brother asks who ate his cookie. What do you do? **a)** Tell him you ate it then laugh. **b)** Tell him you ate it, then apologize. **c)** Tell him that you don't know anything about it.

2. Mom asked you to take the trash out, but you forgot. Later, your mom wonders about it. What do you do? **a)** Pretend you didn't hear her. **b)** Say you asked someone else to do it, although you didn't. **c)** Admit you forgot and take it out.

3. You didn't do your homework. Your teacher asks you where your work is. What do you do? **a)** Tell her you didn't do it and accept the consequences. **b)** Tell her you did it, but forgot it at home. **c)** Tell her you hamster ate it.

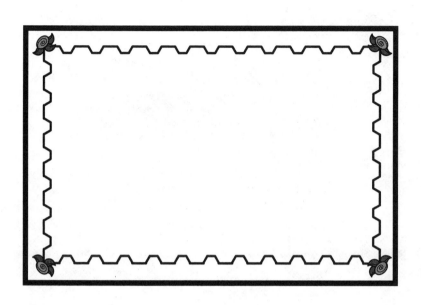

Teabag Tag Pattern

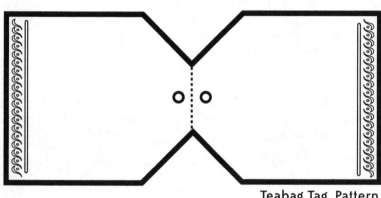

Aa Bb Cc Dd Ee
Ff Gg Hh Ii Jj
Kk Ll Mm Nn
Oo Pp Qq Rr Ss
Tt Uu Vv Ww Xx
Yy Zz

Chapter 4

The kids you teach are part of a greater community—your city, your state or province, and country. Most likely you celebrate Christian holidays such as Christmas and Easter at church with your kids. But what about some of the holidays that come from national experiences or the culture around you? Some of these are great opportunities to pause with your kids and reflect on the influence of Christians on these occasions.

Christian **conviction** motivates some leaders, such as Dr. Martin Luther King, Jr. A Christian **perspective** influences the leadership of others, such as Abraham Lincoln or Billy Graham. A Christian **view of the world** allows all of us to respond to national events and historic occasions in a way that honors God.

When your kids have a day off of school, let that remind you to look for the Godprint in the holiday they're observing. Help kids develop a response to their country or traditions that reflects their belief that God is in control and at the heart of the celebration.

The bulletin boards in this chapter are flexible enough to adapt for national holidays such as Memorial Day, Veteran's Day or a remembrance of September 11. They help connect patriotism and faith on holidays such as Independence Day, Flag Day or Presidents' Day. They honor the convictions of people such as Dr. Martin Luther King, Jr. They also add a reflective element to traditions such as Valentine's Day or Mother's Day.

SO TAKE A LOOK AT THESE WELL SEASONED REASONS TO CELEBRATE WITH YOUR KIDS!

The Dream Marches On

Bible Verse

1 Corinthians 15:58

Therefore, my dear brothers, stand firm. Let nothing move you. Always give yourselves fully to the work of the Lord, because you know that your labor in the Lord is not in vain.

Godprint

conviction

Strong and unshakeable faith in God leads to actions of determination. Real-life examples encourage kids to take action based on their faith in God.

Purpose

THE KIDS WILL LEARN ABOUT THE DREAMS AND CONVICTIONS OF OTHERS AND HOW THEY EXHIBITED STRONG, UNSHAKEABLE FAITH. KIDS WILL COMPARE THE WAY PEOPLE DEMONSTRATE THEIR CONVICTIONS, THEN TUNE INTO THEIR OWN CONVICTIONS AS THEY MARCH ON TO THE BEAT OF GOD.

Get List

- Colored bulletin board paper or old sheet music
- Musical instrument case
- Cardboard
- Construction paper in various colors
- Foil
- String
- Books from the library on band instruments
- Polyester fiberfill
- Reproduce page 77

Construction Site: Make a musical background. The kids will make band instruments to add to this bulletin board.

1 Cover the bulletin board with colorful bulletin board paper or old sheet music.

2 Use construction paper to cut out the title to the bulletin board, "The Dream Marches On." Attach the title to an old instrument case (such as a guitar case). Hang the instrument case from the ceiling just in front of the bulletin board.

3 Cover the top half of the bulletin board with the polyester fiber fill.

Mini Lesson

- What do Abraham Lincoln, Dr. Martin Luther King Jr. and Rev. Billy Graham have in common? *(Let kids speculate.)*
- If I told you they were in the same band, what would you think?

People like Abraham Lincoln, Martin Luther King, Jr. and Billy Graham are famous because they believed in something so much that they couldn't help but take action. In a way, they all played in the same band—we'll call it the "Dream Band." Ask a volunteer to read 1 Corinthians 15:58.

These three people gave themselves fully to the work that God gave them to do. In the "Dream Band" they played different instruments. Abraham Lincoln had a dream to end slavery. He never gave up despite much opposition. We can imagine his determination as a slow and steady drum beat. Martin Luther King, Jr. had a dream to change the way African-American people were treated in the United States. We can imagine his message as a trumpet sound wherever he went, proclaiming the rights of all people. Billy Graham had a dream to turn the world upside down for Jesus. We can imagine his salvation message was a trombone, strong and low, giving a foundation for the eternal melody in the lives of many people.

- Can you think of some other people who believed in something so much that they dreamed of changing the world?

Hand out the "Dream Clouds" from p. 77. **What do you think God's dream is for you? Write or draw on your handout about something that you believe in so much that you want to be in the "Dream Band" to do God's work.** Give kids some time to work. Then glue the clouds in the polyester cloud on the bulletin board.

The people we talked about today were all doing God's work, but they were using different instruments. If you were a band instrument for God, which instrument would you be? Are you a drum that keeps things steady? Or are you a trumpet, which makes a lot of brassy noise? Maybe you're a flute, which enhances the melody? Or perhaps you're a clarinet, which doesn't get a lot of credit but does a lot of the behind-the-scenes work?

Spin-Offs: Here are other examples of people who showed great conviction to the work of God:
- Moses leads God's people (Exodus 3).
- Young Daniel and his friends (Daniel 1).
- Daniel in the lion's den (Daniel 6).
- Saul became Paul and played a new tune (Acts 9).

Choose an instrument that you would be in God's band and have a rootin' tootin' good time making it. Have the kids think of an instrument. Then provide materials such as cardboard and foil for the kids to make their own instruments. Have kids march parade-style around the room tooting or strumming on their instruments. Then attach the instruments to the bulletin board.

- Tell me why you picked the instrument you did.
- Tell me about someone you know who shows great conviction.
- How is a band like all the people who do God's work?

God is the one who gives us the music to play in the "Dream Band." When we listen closely to God, he will help us know the "instrument" he wants us to play in life. And he never gives us the wrong music! We can stand firm in the work of the Lord!

Dream On...
What is God's dream for me?

_____

_____

_____

_____

_____

Dream On...
What is God's dream for me?

_____

_____

_____

_____

_____

Which Path Will You Take?

Godprint

love

When we show love, we show an unselfish concern for the good of another person. We love others because God loves us.

Purpose

USE THIS FUN BULLETIN BOARD GAME TO REINFORCE THE CHARACTERISTICS OF LOVE. HELP KIDS UNDERSTAND THAT THE "EASIEST" PATH IN LIFE ISN'T ALWAYS WHAT IT SEEMS.

Get List

- Valentine's print wrapping paper (or bulletin board paper)
- Stapler
- Construction paper
- Scissors
- Markers
- Shape scissors
- Poster board
- Overhead or opaque projector
- Pencils
- Glue
- Velcro® tabs or strips
- Reproduce page 81
- *Optional: yarn, cloth scraps and other decorative items, clear self-adhesive paper*

Construction Site: Make two inter-connected paths of love that end up at the same point. Kids will play a game to see which is the best path.

1 Cover the bulletin board with a Valentine print wrapping paper or bulletin board paper. Cut out letters for the title of the board. Staple the letters along the top of the bulletin board.

2 From construction paper, cut out at least 13 squares and at least 20 circles to create the pathways. Choose the size that will fill your board nicely. In the center each square or circle, place a 2-inch strip of Velcro®. On one circle write: "The Circle Path—Start Here" On one square write:" The Square Path—Start Here."

3 Cut out a fun-shaped end piece for the pathways or use the heart pattern. Put a 2-inch piece of Vel-cro on this piece. Write: "End! Love one another as I have loved you. John 15:14."

4 Write the sentences from the lists on page 81 on the circles and squares as indicated. If your bulletin board is large and you need more circles or squares to create longer paths, add some of your own ideas. Keep in mind the square path must be shorter. The square path should have mostly "go back" statements so kids will realize it s not the best path to take. The circle path has mostly "positive" statements about demonstrating love. A few circles and squares may be blank.

5 Make two "bridges" using strips of poster board. Staple the bridges onto the bulletin board so that they bow out. Securely staple or glue the circles and squares on the board to create two paths, both using one bridge and ending at the same point. Tape or glue the circles or squares over or under the bridges as needed.

6 Use a ready-made numbered spinner from a board game. Make a pocket to hold the spinner in the upper left-hand corner of the bulletin board. Label the pocket: "Spinner."

7 Have kids create their game pieces (described in the mini lesson).

Mini Lesson

Look at this fun bulletin board! It's actually a big game board for us to use.

- **What is the name of this game?** *(Which Path Will You Take?)*
  - **What clues do you think that title gives us about this game?**

Spin-Offs: Use a bulletin board with a game format to help kids recall facts from Bible stories you've studied together. Put a map background behind the game to review the missionary journeys of Paul. You can also adapt this board to use with these Bible portions:

- Walking a path of integrity, not a crooked path (Proverbs 10:9).
- Esther makes courageous choices (Esther 1–10).

Before we play this game, we each need to make a game piece. Invite kids to make representations of themselves using a 4" x 4" piece of poster board. They can create and cut out their likenesses any way they choose. Place decorative items out for them to use, such as yarn or felt pieces. You may wish to cover the pieces with clear self-adhesie paper for added durability. On the back of each game piece, glue or staple a small Velcro square.

Ask a volunteer to read John 15:12 from a Bible.

Jesus was talking to his disciples when he said this. He knew that he would die, but he wanted his disciples to keep showing love to each other.

- **Let's name some ways that we can show love to other people.**

Invite the kids to place their game pieces on the start piece of either path. **The object of this game is to get to the end.** Point out the end of the paths and the Bible verse. **Everyone who gets to the end is a winner. The rules of this game are simple. First, spin the spinner to see how many spaces you move forward. Then, read the space you've landed on. Do whatever it says.** Show the kids how to carefully stick and remove their pieces to and from the Velcro so they don't pull the spaces off the board.

As you play the game with your kids, discuss each paths' "stones." Ask questions such as: How does this show love to someone? What would have been a better choice? Point out that just as the square path gives us chances to choose a better path, so we also have chances to choose better things in our lives. After everyone finishes, talk about:

- **What happened when you landed on a space that showed a loving choice?** *(You get to stay put; you don't have to move.)*
- **What happened for selfish choices?** *(You have to go back.)*
- **How is that like real life?** *(When you make bad choices in real life, they can hurt you. Having consequences for bad choices is like having to "go back" in the game. A good choice helps others as well as you.)*

Put these statements on circles

- You cheered up your friend when she was sad. You are encouraging!
- You didn't obey your dad. Go back 2.
- You chose to play with a new student. You are friendly!
- You carried papers for your teacher. You are courteous!
- You helped your sister pick up her toys. You are cooperative!
- You gave everyone in class a piece of candy. You are fair!
- You remember to say, "Please" and "Thank you." You are respectful!
- You took your brother's quarter. Go back 2.
- You turned in a quarter you found. You are honest!
- You offered to help a student study to raise his grade. You are generous!
- You smiled at everyone today. You are cheerful!
- You allowed a student to get a drink ahead of you. You are patient!
- You try to help others as much as you can. You are helpful!

Put these statements on squares.

- You helped your mom feed the baby. You are helpful!
- You gave half of your lunch to a friend. You are generous!
- You hit your sister in anger. Go back 2.
- "Choose today whom you will serve." If you'd like to start over on the circle path, go there now.
- You took your neighbor's ball and kept it. Go back 2.
- Feel lost? Last chance! If you'd like to start over on the circle path, go there now.
- You made fun of the new kids during lunch. Go back 2.
- You ignored your mom. Go back 2.
- You didn't let a student play with you. Go back 2.
- You tripped a kid at school. Go back 2.

Respect for Everyone

Bible Verse

1 Peter 2:17

Show proper respect to everyone: Love the brotherhood of believers, fear God, honor the king.

Godprint

respectfulness

All people are precious to God. Because of this, God wants us to treat each other with consideration and respect. He even tells us to show respect for our leaders.

Purpose

KIDS WILL RECOGNIZE THAT GOD WANTS US TO SHOW RESPECT TO EVERYONE, AND HE TELLS US HOW TO DO THAT. THEN THEY'LL LEARN TO EXPRESS SPECIAL APPRECIATION FOR NATIONAL LEADERS.

Get List

- Red, white (and blue for U.S.) bulletin board paper
- Red, white (and blue for U.S.) construction paper
- Scissors
- Tape
- Glue
- Magazines with photographs of national leaders
- White envelopes
- White stationery
- Pencils or pens
- Reproduce patterns on page 85
- *Optional: patriotic stickers, shape scissors*

Construction Site: Create a flag
background. These instructions include options for the flags of the United States and Canada. Kids will add pictures of national leaders and envelopes to hold messages to leaders.

For a United States flag:

1 Cover the bulletin board area with white bulletin board paper. Cut out a large blue square for the flag. Glue or staple it in the upper left-hand corner.

2 Measure the height of your flag bulletin board. Divide by 13 to determine the correct height for each stripe. Cut out seven stripes of red bulletin board paper Create the 13 stripes by stapling or gluing on the red stripes, with white strips in between. The first and last stripes must be red.

3 Copy (and enlarge or reduce if necessary) the star pattern on page 85 onto white paper. Cut out enough stars for the class and set aside for the mini-lesson. If you want to have 50, overlap them when kids put them up on the board.

For a Canadian flag:

1 Cover the bulletin board area with white bulletin board paper.

2 Cut out a large red maple leaf using the diagram on page 85 as a pattern. Staple the maple leaf in the center of the bulletin board. Copy (and enlarge or reduce if necessary to fit your board) the maple leaf so you have enough for all the kids.

3 Staple two red rectangles on either end of the bulletin board.

Continue for both flags:

4 Cut letters from red or blue construction paper for the title, "Respect for Everyone." Attach the title to the top of the bulletin board.

5 Add the words of the Bible verse to the bottom stripe or another portion of the flag. "Show proper respect to everyone: Love the brotherhood of believers, fear God, honor the king" (1 Peter 2:17).

6 If you choose, decorate with patriotic stickers. Staple or glue onto one of the white stripes or above the maple leaf.

Mini Lesson

You can use this lesson to honor current national leaders, past leaders or even world leaders.

As kids gather, greet them with a deep bow. Call them "sir" or "ma'am." Go out of your way to treat them with deference and respect.

Spin-Offs: Use this patriotic bulletin board for Independence Day. Have the kids write letters or poems telling why they appreciate their country and freedom. You can also adapt this board to use with this verse:

• The elders who direct the affairs of the church are worthy of double honor, especially those who preach and teach (1 Timothy 5:17).

• **What does it mean when we bow to someone?** *(Show respect; show that we know that person is important or in charge.)*
• **Let's think of ways to show respect to other people.**
• **Who are some people to whom you show respect?**

God tells us just how to show respect. Ask a volunteer to read 1 Peter 2:17 from a Bible.

• **What are three ways this verse says to show respect?** *(Love the brotherhood of believers; fear God; honor the king.)*
• **Which of these three do you think is hardest to do? Why?**
• **Do we have to honor a king for the third one to apply to us? Explain.**

Every country has leaders. We have leaders for our town, for our state (or province) and for our country. God wants us to honor our leaders and show them respect.

Draw kids' attention to the flag you've prepared on the bulletin board. **Our flag looks a little bare. Let's show respect for our leaders and finish the bulletin board. First we'll look through these magazines for pictures of our leaders and add them to the board.** U.S. flags: Have kids cut out pictures of leaders, glue them to stars and add the stars to the blue square. Canadian flags: Kids can glue pictures to maple leaves and attach them to the red portions of the flag. For either flag, talk about the leaders you want to honor, whether current leaders or others who have contributed to the country's history in some way. Make sure that the magazines you provide have pictures of the people you're honoring.

The second thing we'll do is write letters of appreciation to our leaders. Use the "I Appreciate You!" letter and fill in the blanks with your own message. Then put your message in an envelope and add it to the board. If you're making a U.S. flag, have kids add the envelopes to the red stripes. Make sure the flaps face out and remain open. If you're making a Canadian flag, add envelopes to the white portion around the maple leaf.

When you're finished with the board you can mail the letters to appropriate individuals. Or you can have kids address their own envelopes in a follow-up class.

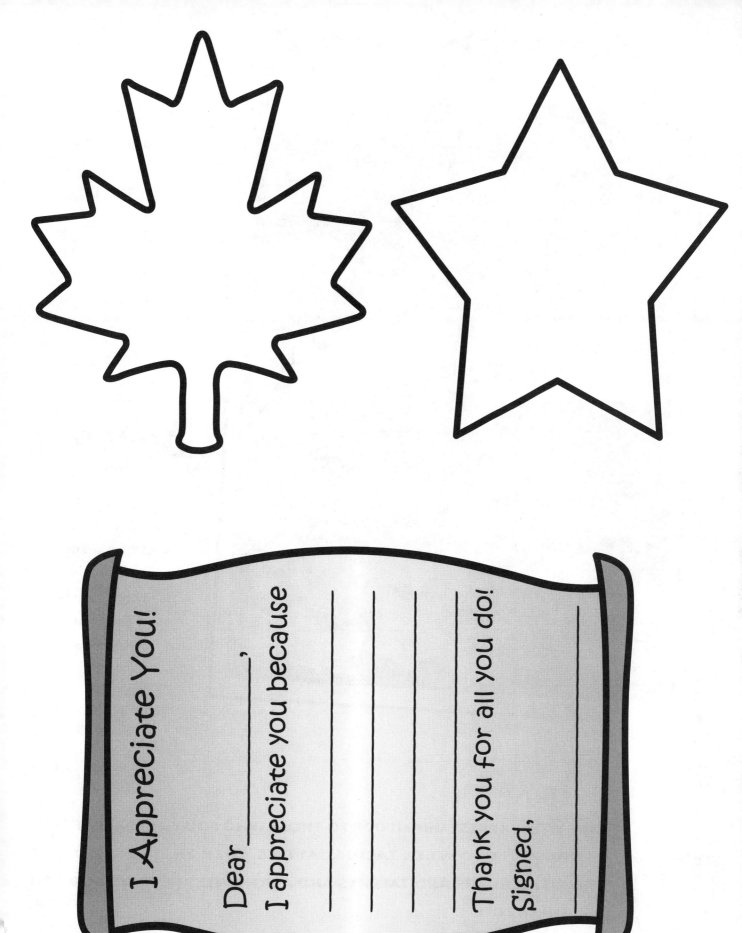

I Appreciate You!

Dear _____ ,

I appreciate you because _____

_____

_____

Thank you for all you do!

Signed,

Superheroes!

Bible Verse

1 Corinthians 16:13

Be on your guard; stand firm in the faith; be men of courage; be strong.

Godprint

courage

Lead kids into the discovery of superhero strength only found in God to stand firm in the face of danger or persecution.

Purpose

KIDS WILL EXPRESS GRATITUDE TO THOSE WHO FOUND STRENGTH AND COURAGE IN GOD WHEN FACING BATTLES. THEN THEY'LL CELEBRATE THEIR STRENGTHS AND TALENTS AND ACKNOWLEDGE WAYS GOD CAN USE THEM, TOO.

Get List

- Red and white bulletin board paper
- Red, white (and blue) streamers
- Black and white construction paper
- Books on history from the local library
- Copy paper
- Stapler
- Markers
- Bibles
- Reproduce page 89
- *Optional: blue bulletin board paper*

Construction Site:

Construct three different sections to this board. The first section focuses on national heroes. The middle section is about how God can use the strengths kids have. The last section is about heroes of faith.

1 Divide the bulletin board into three equal sections. Cover the first section with red bulletin board paper, the second with white and the third section with red again. If you prefer, use blue on the third section.

2 Use the black construction paper to cut out the title of the bulletin board, "Superheroes." Staple the title across the top of the bulletin board.

3 In the first red section, use the black paper to make the title, "Memory Lane" and attach the the title to the middle of the section. Make the title, "Heroes of Today," for the white section and "Heroes of Faith" for the final section.

Mini Lesson

Kids will make additions to the three sections for the bulletin board. You might prefer to have kids help you build the bulletin board over a three-week period, constructing one section each week.

- **What is courage?**
- **Can you give me examples of people you know who have shown courage?** *(Give the kids time to discuss the topic of courage.)*

We're going to take a closer look at people who have shown courage and see what we can learn from these superheroes.

Section 1 (Red)
Many people have given their time and lives defending this nation and other nations that stand for freedom. Some of these people trusted God for the strength to do this. Let's honor these men and women with a great big salute.

Hand out the books from the library. **Use these books to find a hero whom you would like to honor.** Hand out the copy paper, white construction paper and markers. **On the** copy paper, draw a picture of the hero you choose to thank. If you're using this bulletin board to observe a particular national holiday, you can give more specific suggestions for what you'd like kids to draw. **Then glue the picture onto a construction paper frame. Fill out a flag** (page 89) **and tape it below the picture on the bulletin board.** Have the kids add the pictures and the flags to the bulletin board. **Let's take a walk down memory lane.** Have the children share their drawings and the information they discovered about their superheroes.

• **Why is it important to remember our national heroes?**

Spin-Offs: Use this bulletin board to focus on characteristics that make heroes. Or and look at how God uses our weaknesses and gives us strength. You can use this concept with these passages:

• Heroes of the Faith (Hebrews 11).

Section 2 (White)

Let's feature the courageous people of today—people who face the dangers of life every day. And that would be you! You have strengths that God can use to help you be courageous in tough times. And God has strength he wants to give you. Ask a volunteer to read 1 Corinthians 16:13.

• **What kinds of things do we need to be on guard against?**
• **Where does our courage come from?**
• **How can ordinary people be heroes?**

God asks you to be his superheroes. And he's there to help you be strong and to have courage. Draw a picture of yourself, a superhero for God, on the white copy paper. Kids can make comic drawings of themselves. Have them glue drawings to a construction paper frame. Then have them fill out "flying" superheroes from the reproducible. Display these on the bulletin board. You might wish to pause and have the kids pray, thanking God for being with them through the good times and the tough times.

Section 3 (Red or Blue)

God gives people superhero strength through every age. The Bible is full of stories of superheroes of faith. We can read about people who have been on their guard; people who stood firm in their faith; men and women of courage (1 Corinthians 16:13). Look through the Bible and choose a person who faced a challenge with God's help. Have the kids draw a picture of the Bible character on the copy paper. Glue the picture onto a construction paper frame. Then have kids fill out a reproduced "Bible" to go with the superhero of faith. You might wish to have the kids share all that they've learned about their Bible superheroes.

• **What does it mean to "stand firm in the faith"?**
• **How are the people in the Bible examples of courage for today?**

A BIG HERO SALUTE

TO: _____

HOW DID HE OR SHE SHOW COURAGE?

THANK YOU FOR:

A BIG HERO SALUTE!

HOW DID HE OR SHE SHOW COURAGE?

THANK YOU FOR...

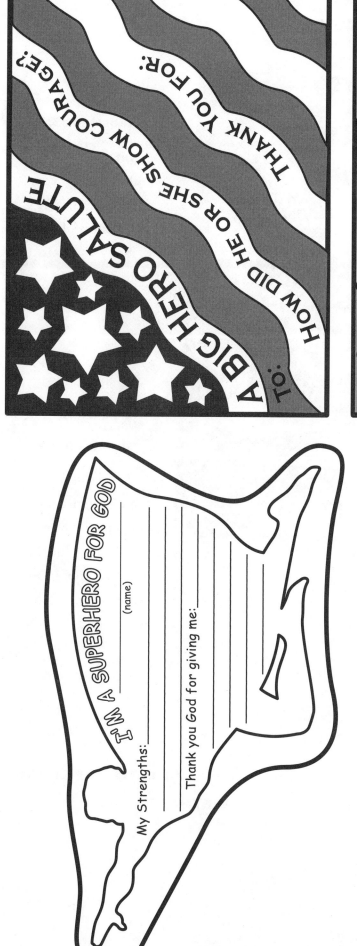

I'M A SUPERHERO FOR GOD

_____
(name)

My Strengths: _____

Thank you God for giving me: _____

Superhero

How did he or she show courage?
_____

B
I
B
L
E

Thank you, God,
for teaching me
about _____

What did God do to
help His superhero?
_____

Let's Talk Turkey

Let the peace of Christ rule in your hearts, since as members of one body you were called to peace. And be thankful.

Godprint
thankfulness

God loves us and acts in ways that are for our good. He wants us to be thankful and show our appreciation for what he does for us and through other people.

Purpose
KIDS WILL EXPRESS THANKFULNESS TO GOD AND TO IMPORTANT PEOPLE IN THEIR LIVES WITH THIS FUN BULLETIN BOARD.

Get List

- Dyed feathers, approximately 8 inches long
- Toothpicks
- 3- to 4-inch Styrofoam® balls
- Brown markers or tempera paint
- Brown, yellow and red chenille wires
- Green construction paper
- Wiggle craft eyes
- Large brown pompons
- Glue
- Tape
- Markers
- Bulletin board paper in green and other colors
- Stapler
- Scissors
- Hot glue gun
- Reproduce the feather on page 93

Construction Site: Prepare a festive background and kids will add a flock of turkeys.

1 Ccover the bulletin board with bulletin board paper. Cut out letters from construction paper to make the board's title, "Let's Talk Turkey!" Staple the title along the top of the board.

2 Measure the length of the board. Cut a piece of green bulletin board paper the same length as teh board and about 1' high. Fringe the top edge of the green paper to resemble grass. Write the Bible verse on the "grass" paper. Staple the grass along the bottom edge of the bulletin board.

3 Prepare the supplies kids will need to make turkeys. Make poster board templates of the 4" feather pattern on page 93. Cut the Styrofoam ball in half so each child gets one-half of a ball. A bread knife works well to cut the balls.

4 Each child will need two 6" pieces of brown chenille wire for the turkey wings; two 3-inch pieces of brown for the legs; one 3" piece of red for wattle; and one 4" piece of yellow for the beak. Give each child six 8" colored feathers and one large brown pompon.

5 Help kids follow these steps to make the turkey. Use the diagram on page 93 as a guide.

a. Use brown markers or paint to color the rounded side of each Styrofoam ball. Paint will soak in, so the color may not be solid.

b. Glue the pompom along the top edge of the ball. Hot glue two craft eyes onto the pompom.

c. Bend the chenille wires into the correct shapes shown on the diagram. Push the wires into the ball as shown. Glue the ends of the beak into the pompom.

d. Trace the feather templates onto construction paper in several colors and cut out the paper feathers.

e. Label one side of each paper feather with the name of the person to whom the feather will go. On the reverse side, have the children write this sentence and complete it: Dear _____, I am thankful for _____. Love, _____

f. Tape a toothpick onto the feather.

g. Along the back top edge of the turkey's body, push the real feathers into the body. Just in front of the real feathers, press the paper feathers into the turkey's body. Turn the paper feathers so that the names show outward.

Dear _____,
I'm thankful for,_____
_____
Love,_____

6 Cut pieces of green construction paper in half so that each child gets a piece. Show kids how to fringe the top edge so that it resembles grass. Have each child write his or her name on the grass.

7 Use a dab of hot glue on the flat back of each turkey to secure them to the bulletin board. Staple the grass name-labels under the appropriate turkeys.

Mini Lesson

• **What holiday are we about to celebrate?** *(Thanksgiving.)*
• **Tell me what Thanksgiving is all about.** *(People taking the time to especially thank God and others for everything they've done or provided for us.)*

The Bible tells us that we should be thankful all of the time. But we especially think about being thankful around this time of year. Ask a volunteer to read Colossians 3:15.

• **What do you think Paul meant when he wrote we are "members of one body?"** *(That we're all a part of the body of Christ; the Church.)*

We are all a part of the Church. We're all important. God uses people to bless other people, doesn't he?

• **Tell me about a time someone blessed you.**
• **What about a time God used you to bless someone else?**

We know that God uses people to bless other people, too. So let's practice this verse! We can be thankful and bless other people all at the same time! Think about the people in your family or here in your church family you're really thankful for. Maybe you appreciate the things they do for everyone. Maybe you're grateful for things they do just for you. Allow for some think-time.

Let's make a "Thankfulness Turkey." On the turkeys we'll put feathers of thankfulness for the people we want to thank and bless. Create the turkeys and bulletin board as described in the Construction Site section of this lesson.

Make sure to give parents or other church members an opportunity to "pluck" a feather that may be waiting just for them!

> **Spin-Offs:** Have the children write one thing they're thankful for on each paper feather. Use the paper feathers for members in each child's family or for church leaders. Create "thankfulness flowers" in the same manner, making the flowers' petals the note to share. You can also adapt this board for these stories:
>
> • Jesus blesses people with healing miracles (assorted passages from the Gospels).
> • Jesus heals ten people with leprosy, one is thankful (Luke 17:11–19).

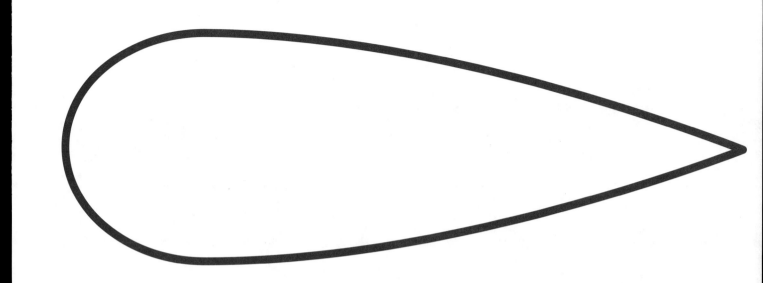

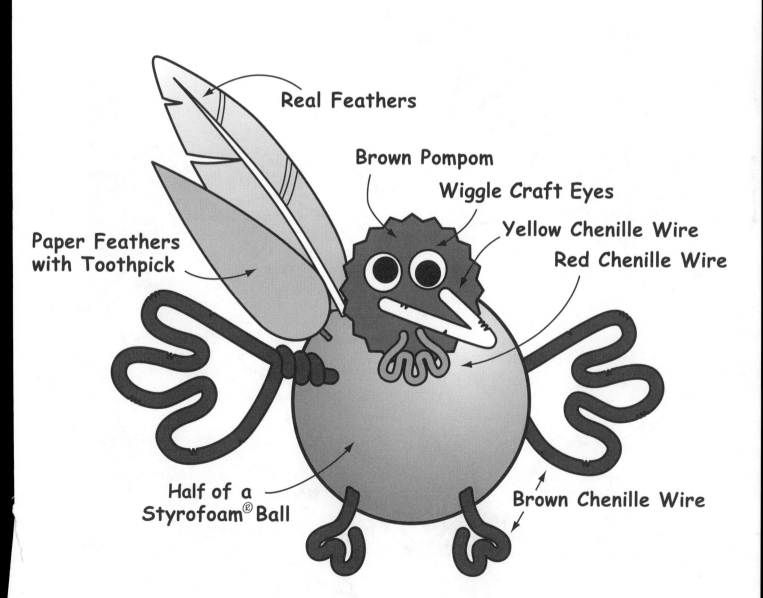

Real Feathers

Brown Pompom

Wiggle Craft Eyes

Yellow Chenille Wire
Red Chenille Wire

Paper Feathers
with Toothpick

Half of a
Styrofoam® Ball

Brown Chenille Wire

Chapter 5

"What if I don't have a permanent bulletin board?"

Portability becomes an issue when you borrow or share space and you can't have custody of the bulletin board on a permanent basis. No problem. You may not have permanent space, but that doesn't mean you can't teach *off the wall*. It means that you might teach from a hanging shower curtain or bed sheet. You might put a bulletin board on the back of an old banner or hammer together some boards and set them on the floor. Visit a hobby store and make a portable bulletin board from foam core display boards and plastic hinges that snap together. The right kind of tag-alongs can be rolled up, tossed in a box or folded up. With a little imagination, you can still teach *off the wall*—or the floor, or the ceiling!

You can also use Tag-alongs as interactive activity centers. Perhaps you have time to fill as kids trickle into class. Set up your Tag-along and let the kids have fun creating and learning. Tag-alongs may not have physical permanence in your classroom, but they can certainly leave a permanent impact on your kids.

TAG-ALONGS CAN BE ROLLED UP, FOLDED UP OR OSSED IN A BOX.

Tune Your 'Tude

TUNE YOUR 'TUDE

I know, my God, that you test the heart and are pleased with integrity.
1 Chronicles 29:17

Bible Verse

1 Chronicles 29:17

I know, my God, that you test the heart and are pleased with integrity.

Godprint

integrity

Kids make choices every day. As they grow in knowing God, they learn to make choices that show that they are new creations in Christ Jesus.

Purpose

THIS FUN BULLETIN BOARD ENCOURAGES KIDS TO DEMONSTRATE THE GODLY CHARACTERISTICS OF PEOPLE IN THE BIBLE. INVITE THE KIDS TO "TUNE THE RADIO" TO A STATION THAT DISPLAYS POSITIVE BEHAVIOR AND CHARACTERISTICS.

Get List

- Blank hangable banner or shower curtain
- Large cereal box
- Markers
- Metal brad
- Long straw
- Glue
- Stapler
- Construction or self-adhesive paper
- Poster board
- Double-sided tape
- Small Styrofoam® ball
- Silver paint
- Reproduce page 99

Construction Site: Build a radio.

Kids will turn dials to match clues with a Bible character.

1 Cover a cereal box with self-adhesive paper or construction paper. Cut an 8″ (or larger) slit into the top of the cereal box. Cut a 4″ slit along the bottom end of the box near the front edge. Cut two horizontal 4″ lines on the front of the box, near the bottom edge, two inches apart. Make sure all three slits align.

2 Cut an 8″ (or larger) circle of poster board. Decorate the circle and divide it into four "pie" segments with some space in between. Write the following text in the pie-shaped boxes on the circle.

Section 1: I stay true to what I believe. I'll stick by you through thick and thin.
Section 2: I feel deeply for others. I know how you're feeling and I'd like to help.
Section 3: If I have something you need, you can use it or have it. I love to share with others.
Section 4: I'll stand brave knowing God is with me no matter what. When others might run away, I won't.

On the front of the box near the top, cut a pie-shaped opening that matches the size of the pie segments on your circle. You may wish to use a tracing-paper pattern of your circle.

3 Copy the wide strip on page 99. Glue the strip onto a 4″ x 9″ piece of poster board. Decorate it if you wish.

4 Turn the box on its side, with the "pie" hole on the left and the slits on the right. Place the circle in the 8″ slit so that part of the circle is showing outside of the box and a pie segment shows through the hole. Attach the circle to the box with a metal brad. Weave the strip through the slits and cut along the bottom end of the box so that the text shows.

5 Use markers to draw on knobs and dials to make the box look like a radio. Use rubber cement to attach the box to the center of your bulletin board. Create an antenna for the

radio using a straw and a small Styrofoam® ball. Paint them silver.

6 Create two female and two male character faces. Use yarn, felt, wiggle eyes or other objects to add dimension. Fold four pieces of heavy construction paper in half. Photocopy and enlarge the clue boxes on page 99. On the inside of each folded piece of construction paper, write the character's name and characteristic he or she displayed. On the outside, affix the clue box. Display the characters and cards around the bulletin board.

> I died just for you so that you and I could live together forever. Read about me in John 3:16

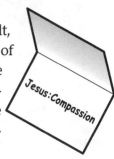
Jesus: Compassion

Mini Lesson

Invite the kids to sit in a large circle. **Let's learn a new rhyme and rhythm.** Begin a slow rhythm of two thigh-slaps then two hand-claps. Begin saying the rhyme one line at a time:

In-teg-ri-ty! (Repeat.) **In-teg-ri-ty!** (Repeat.)
Liv-ing like God (Repeat.) **Wants me to be.** (Repeat.)
There's hon-e-sty! (Repeat.) **Gen-er-os-ity!** (Repeat.)
And don't forget, (Repeat.) **There's loy-al-ty!** (Repeat.)
I choose to be (Repeat.) **Full of in-tegrity!** (Repeat.)

Integrity. That's a rather hard word. What does integrity mean to you? Pause for answers. **Integrity means to live a life like Jesus did. Jesus lived in a way that showed that he was close to God. That's how God wants us to live.**

Many people in the Bible are examples of integrity. Can anyone think of someone in the Bible who lived in a way that showed that he or she was close to God? *(Noah was obedient; Zacchaeus became honest; Abraham was full of integrity; Moses was humble; Ruth was loyal; Lazarus was thankful.)* Ask a volunteer to read the first part of 1 Chronicles 29:17: "I know my God, that you test the heart and are pleased with integrity."

• **How does God feel about integrity?**
• **Why do you think integrity is important?**

Spin-Offs: This radio can be used to match up different riddles and answers for all sorts of lessons such as: Old Testament/New Testament books of the Bible; Bible Verses and their references; biblical characters and their deeds. You can also adapt this concept to use with these Bible stories:

• David shows integrity when he doesn't take revenge on Saul (1 Samuel 24:1–20).
• Joseph acts with integrity toward Mary (Matthew 1:18–2:15).

Let's look at this bulletin board called Tune Your 'Tude. This bulletin board will help us see the right attitudes (or characteristics) to live. Show the kids how to "tune" the radio to match the characteristic and its definition, then find the biblical character who showed that characteristic.

If we live lives full of integrity, we show the world a true picture of who Jesus is. Let's decide now to live lives full of integrity.

PUSH OR PULL GENTLY

COMPASSION

COURAGE

LOYALTY

GENEROSITY

PUSH OR PULL GENTLY

I stayed with my mother-in-law and moved to her homeland, even when my husband had died. I gathered grain so we both could eat.
Read about me in
Ruth 1:1-4:12

Ruth:Loyalty

I kept on praying to God, even when praying became illegal. I trusted God to keep me safe when I was put in with a bunch of hungry lions.
Read about me in
Daniel 6:1-28

Daniel:Courage

I supplied David and his army with food and drink, even when my husband refused to do so.
Read about me in
1 Samuel 25:1-35

Abigail:Generosity

I was traveling on a road to Jericho. I found a man who had been robbed and helped him.
Read about me in
Luke 10:30-35

Good Samaritan:
Compassion

Compassion E.R.

BibleVerse
Isaiah 61:1

The LORD has anointed me to preach good news to the poor. He has sent me to bind up the brokenhearted.

Godprint
compassion

Help the kids discover another's need, particularly during times of distress or unhappiness and instill in them the desire to respond with God's love.

Purpose

KIDS WILL EXPLORE WHAT CAUSES A WOUNDED HEART. THEN THEY WILL THINK OF WAYS TO SHOW COMPASSION AND HELP BROKEN-HEARTED PEOPLE.

Get List

___ Tri-fold poster board
___ Medical paraphernalia: masks, bandages, stethoscopes, green scrubs, hats, shoes
___ Green bulletin board paper
___ Construction paper
___ Small zip-top bags
___ Red hair gel
___ Newspaper
___ Plastic Garbage bags
___ Chair
___ Balloon
___ Red poster board
___ Hot glue gun and glue sticks
___ Red glitter glue
___ Reproduce page 103

Construction Site: Make a board that has a wounded heart in the center of it.

1 Stuff garbage bags with newspaper and arrange them to represent the torso, arms and legs of a person. Dress the person in medical scrubs. Use a balloon for the head. Place a chair by the bulletin board and put the person in it. If you pull the back of the shirt over the back of the chair, he'll sit up.

2 Cover the board with green bulletin board paper. Then attach all of the medical paraphernalia to the left and right sides of the board. Cut out letters for the title, "Compassion E.R."

3 In the center of the board, add a wounded heart. Cut a large heart from red poster board. Then cut a small four-inch by four-inch heart out of the center of the large heart. Fill a zip-top bag with 1/2 cup of red gel. Zip the bag closed and tape the edges together to be sure it's sealed. Position the bag behind the large heart so that it shows through the window and tape it down. On the back of the large heart, tape all the edges of the zip-top bag tautly behind the small heart opening. Attach the large heart to the bulletin board.

Mini Lesson

How many of you have been to an Emergency Room? Give the kids time to share about their experiences.

People who work in an Emergency Room show compassion and care for people who are hurting. It's their job and they get paid to do their job. Did you know that God wants us to be E.R. workers too? That's right. He wants us to care and show compassion to those whose hearts are hurting.

Read the portion of Isaiah 61:1 for this lesson: "The LORD has anointed me to preach good news to the poor. He has sent me to bind up the brokenhearted."

• What does "brokenhearted" mean?
• What does God want us to do for people with wounded hearts?

Healing wounded hearts by showing compassion and telling others about Jesus is one of the jobs that God has given us. We don't get paid in money, but we do get paid by knowing that we are pleasing God.

How do people get wounded hearts? Let's think about things that would hurt the hearts of people. *(Name calling, teasing, someone dies, someone is hurt, get yelled at, blamed for something you didn't do.)*

Spin-Offs: You can use this bulletin board with stories about Bible characters who showed compassion:

• The Good Samaritan (Luke 10).
• Paul shows compassion to his shipmates (Acts 27).
• Jesus shows compassion for Zacchaeus (Luke 19).

Hand out the reproducible hearts. Have the kids write their ideas on the hearts. Kids can add red glitter glue to the hearts to emphasize that they're wounded hearts. Add the hearts to the bulletin board.

Showing compassion helps heal their wounded hearts. Telling others about Jesus is sometimes the only way we can help heal a wounded heart. But there are other helpful things that we can do to show compassion to those whose hearts are wounded. What are some things you can do to show compassion?

Hand out the strip and circle bandages. Have the kids write ways that they can show compassion and put them on the board next to the wounded hearts. You might choose to have the kids write two or three bandages for each wounded heart on the board.

• How do you know that someone's heart is hurting?
• When you see that someone else's heart is hurting, how does your heart feel?
• Tell me about someone who has shown compassion to you.

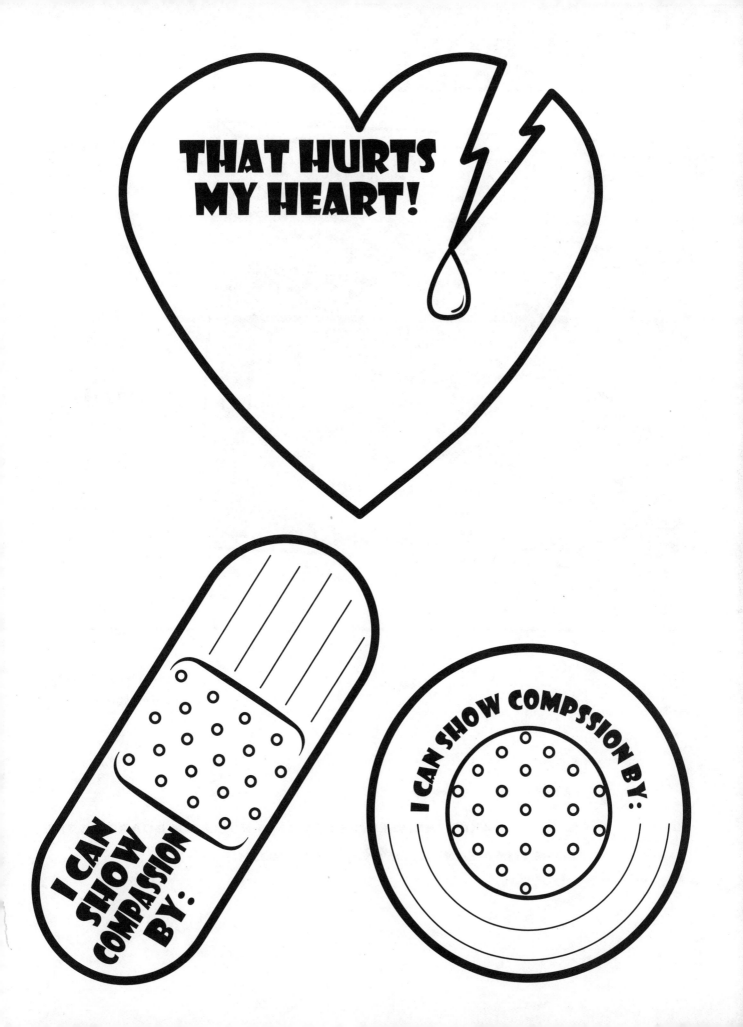

Faithful Friends

Godprint

friendliness

Elementary-age kids choose their own friends more and more. They're ready to learn that friendliness means showing interest in building a two-way relationship with another person, just as we have a two-way relationship with God.

Purpose

KIDS WILL "MAKE" THEMSELVES FOR THIS BULLETIN BOARD AS THEY EXPLORE THE MEANING OF GODLY FRIENDSHIP.

Get List

- Double-stick tape
- Construction paper
- Scissors
- Markers
- Poster board
- Pencils
- Glue
- Reproduce the Faithful Friends pattern on page 107
- *Optional: yarn, cloth, buttons, scraps, chenille wires, craft sticks, cotton balls, dried leaves or flowers, Easter grass, other decorative items desired*

Construction Site: Construct a playground; then the kids will add themselves to the picture.

1 Cut out letters to create the title of the bulletin board. Tape or glue the title along the top of the bulletin board. Make a sign for the Bible verse and reference. Tape or glue the sign along the bottom of the bulletin board.

2 Use supplies provided to create the background for the bulletin board that includes activities kids enjoy, such as swinging, swimming, reading, climbing a tree, or playground equipment. Use bulletin board paper for grass, hills and sky. Use construction paper for things such as trees or a swimming pool. Make water from crumpled blue cellophane. Use chenille wires to create a goalpost or a swing set. Easter grass can be glued on to add life-like grass to the board. You might like to have them help you make the playground.

3 Reproduce the pattern on page 107. Kids will use these as patterns to make "Faithful Friends." Kids can cut out and decorate these shapes, or they can use these as patterns to cut shapes out of poster board or construction paper.

Mini Lesson

Everyone think of a really good friend. What is it about him or her that makes a good friend? Invite kids to share.

• What are some things that you like to do with your friends? *(If kids give answers that are represented on your bulletin board, point them out.)*

As kids answer, make a list in a visible place that they can refer to later. Some ideas to be sure to add are: sharing, cooperative, honest, kind, fair, dependable, understanding, respectful, patient, flexible, generous.

Those are some great ideas. I wrote some of them down. Being a good friend isn't always easy, is it? For example.... Share an experience from your own life, such as a time when you did what a friend wanted to do rather than what you preferred.

In Proverbs 17:17, the Bible says, "A friend loves at all times."

• Is it easy or hard to love your friends all the time? Why?
• How can you show love to your friends?

Hand out the Faithful Friend from page 107. **We made a list of characteristics that good friends have. We're going to make Faithful Friends to put on our bulletin board. Choose six of these words that you would like to use to describe yourself. Write one word on each main section of your Faithful Friend. Then decorate your Faithful Friend anyway you'd like—to look like you or to look like a friend.**

Spin-Offs: Invite kids to make speech balloons to place on the bulletin board. They can say their favorite "friend" Bible verse, or a positive statement about friendship. You can use the Faithful Friends bulletin board with these stories:

• David and Jonathan are friends (1 Samuel 18–20).
• Four friends bring a paralytic to Jesus (Mark 2:3–12).

Kids can use whatever supplies you have available to embellish their projects, such as yarn for hair, cloth for clothing, buttons for eyes, etc. Invite the kids to use the supplies for extras such as a book or a football in their friend's hands.

Let's put ourselves in this great looking playground! Where would you like to put your Faithful Friend on this bulletin board? If you have extra supplies, kids can also add more activities to the bulletin board itself. Help the kids tape their friends onto the board. Once all the friends are taped on, allow each child to tell about his or her Faithful Friend. Prompt the kids to share by asking questions, such as:

• **What six characteristics did you choose? Why?**
• **Tell us why you placed your friend there.**
• **Tell us why you chose to dress your friend the way you did.**

Building on Books of the Bible

Building on Books of the Bible

We ought therefore to show hospitality to such men so that we may work together for the truth. 3 John 1:8

Genesis · Exodus · Leviticus · Numbers · Deuteronomy · Joshua · Judges · Ruth · 1 Samuel · 2 Samuel · 1 Kings

2 Kings · 1 Chronicles · 2 Chronicles · Ezra · Nehemiah · Esther · Job · Psalms · Proverbs · Ecclesiastes · Song of Songs

Isiah · Jeremiah · Lamentations · Ezekiel · Daniel · Hosea · Joel · Amos · Obadiah · Jonah · Micah

Nahum · Habbakuk · Zephaniah · Haggai · Zechariah · Malachi · Matthew · Mark · Luke · John · Acts

Romans · 1 Corinthians · 2 Corinthians · Galatians · Ephesians · Phillipians · Colossians · 1 Thessalonians · 2 Thessalonians · 1 Timothy · 2 Timothy

Titus · Philemon · Hebrews · James · 1 Peter · 2 Peter · 1 John · 2 John · 3 John · Jude · Revelations

Bible Verse

3 John 8

We ought therefore to show hospitality to such men so that we may work together for the truth.

Godprint

cooperation

Kids are independent and like to have their own way! But they also like to be with other kids. Help them learn to work together toward a common goal that is pleasing to God.

Purpose

PUTTING THE BOOKS OF THE BIBLE IN ORDER WILL GIVE KIDS AN EXPERIENCE OF WORKING TOGETHER AND COOPERATING TO MEET A COMMON GOAL.

Get List

- Large sheet of yellow bulletin board paper approximately 7' x 3'
- Blue and green construction paper
- Brick pattern from p. 111
- Dictionaries
- Bibles
- Plasti-Tak®

Construction Site: Make a "brick wall" of the books of the Bible. When it's finished, you can roll it up and store it easily, hang it from a wall, or lay it on the floor.

1 Lay out the bulletin board paper horizontally. At the top write: "Building on Books of the Bible." Below the title, add the words of the Bible verse.

2 Use the brick pattern on page 111 to cut bricks. Cut a total of 78 bricks from blue construction paper and 54 bricks from the green construction paper. Divide each color set into two piles. Put green and blue bricks together so you have two sets, and each set has 39 blue (Old Testament) and 27 green (New Testament) bricks. Set one set aside for now. Lay out the other set on the yellow paper. Arrange them in rows. Six rows of 11 bricks should fit. Or you can have three rows with 16 bricks and the fourth row with 18 bricks. Glue them onto the yellow bulletin board paper. Draw or shade in around all the bricks to make the project look like a wall of brick and mortar.

3 Now use the other set of bricks. Write the name of a Bible book on each loose brick. The Old Testament books go on the blue bricks and the New Testament books go on the green bricks. Now you should have 66 blank bricks on the wall and 66 loose bricks with the books of the Bible written on them.

Mini Lesson

Before the lesson, hang the brick wall or lay it on the floor. Put the pile of loose bricks several feet away from the wall and mix the blue and green bricks together.

Hand out the dictionaries. **Let's have a little fun with the dictionary. Everyone look up the word "share."** Have the first child or group who finds the word read the definition. **Now look up the word "care."** Have the first child or group who finds the word read the definition.

What helps you find the word quickly? *(Knowing the alphabet.)* **Knowing the alphabet really helps when looking up a word in the dictionary.**

Hand out the Bibles. **Everyone look up the book of Zechariah.** Have the first person who finds it stand. Have everyone give him or her a great big cheer. **Now let's look up 3 John.**

- **What helps you find the books of the Bible?**

The books of the Bible are not in alphabetical orde, but God's Word is in a specific order known as the "Books of the Bible." Let's all read 3 John 8: "We ought therefore to show hospitality to such men so that we may work together for the truth."

- **What does "hospitality" mean?** *(A friendly and generous way of treating others, especially guests. Some kids may want to look the word up in a dictionary.)*
- **What does hospitality have to do with working together?** *(When we work together, we should be friendly and generous.)*

The Bible tells us God's truth. Let's work together to help each other learn the order of the books of the Bible. Knowing the order of the books of the Bible will make it easier for you to find what you're looking for in the Bible.

Show the kids the brick wall. **This is a bare brick wall. Together you're going to build this wall with bricks that have the Books of the Bible written on them. Each person can only carry one brick at a time to the wall. When you get to the wall, put the bricks in the order of the Books of the Bible. Put the loose brick on top of one of the bricks already on the wall.** If your brick wall is on the floor, kids can just set the loose brick on top of the glued down brick. If you hang the brick wall on a bulletin board or classroom wall, use Plasti-Tak® to attach the loose bricks.

- **Can you think of some ways to work together to get this job done?** *(Encourage the kids to come up with a cooperative plan for getting the bricks moved and placed in the proper order.)*

Kids will run back and forth from the wall to the pile of bricks. You might wish to time the group to see if they can reduce the amount of time it takes them to rebuild the wall each time they put it together. For beginners you might wish to start with either the Old or the New Testament and work your way up to the entire Bible. Emphasize teamwork and cooperation.

- **How many books are in the Bible? How many books are in the New Testament? The Old Testament?**
- **What makes it easy for everyone to work together? What makes it challenging?**

Spin-Offs: You could make two sets of bricks and have teams compete against each other. Teams could win based on which team completed the task the fastest or cooperated the best. Or teams could win based on whether everyone knows the order of the books of the Bible. Kids could also make their own set of bricks to take home for practice. You can also use this activity to help kids think about these verses:

- Psalm 119:11: I have hidden your word in my heart that I might not sin against you.
- Deuteronomy 6:6–7: These commands that I give you today are to be upon your hearts. Impress them on your children. Talk about them when you sit at home and when you walk along the road, when you lie down and when you get up.

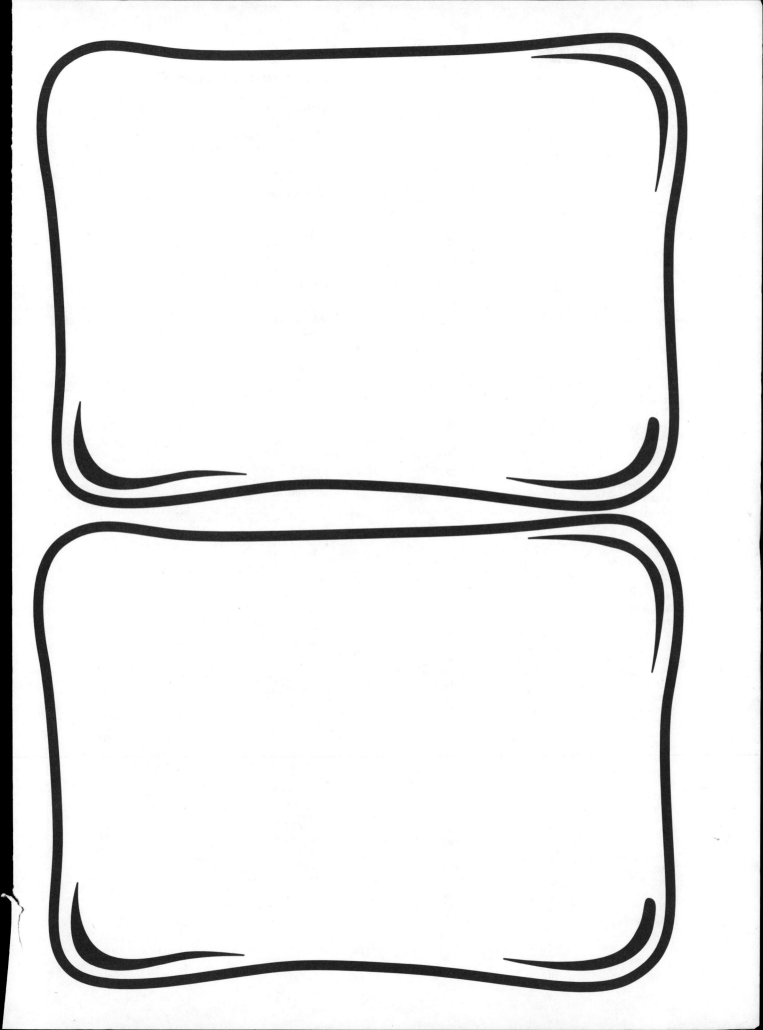

Index

Index of Scripture Passages